my Mi

Man~~~

my Ministry
Manual

by Rev. Gerald
Ambulance

with STEPHEN TOMKINS

Published in Great Britain in 2002 by
Society for Promoting Christian Knowledge
Holy Trinity Church
Marylebone Road
London NW1 4DU

British Library Cataloguing-in-Publication Data
A catalogue record for this book is available from the British Library

ISBN 0-281-05493-2

Typeset by FiSH Books, London WC1
Printed in Great Britain by Bookmarque Ltd, Croydon, Surrey

Contents

Meet the Rev.

A great man of God once said, 'You don't need an appointment to get the Lord's anointment.' It was me! That's the kind of thing this book is all about – deep holy wisdom from above, in easy-to-swallow gobbets.

If you are a man with a ministry (or a woman these days!) this book is for you. (When I say 'or a woman' I mean 'If you are a woman with a ministry', of course. If you are a man with a woman, get your filthy hands off my book.)

Let me start again. Whom is this book for?

(a) Anointed ministers, famous Christians and soul-saving supersonic spiritual celebrities, my beloved yoke-fellows in the egg of Christian ministry. Yes, the

Lord has blessed you unto a mighty work, but which of us can say that we know it all, that we have reached the end of our pilgrimage, and learnt all there is to learn? Me! So read and feed.

(b) Unanointed ministers, C-list spiritual celebrities and part-timers in the fields of worship, youth work, etc. You labour faithfully in the vineyards of Zion, without revivals and miracles, or fame and riches. Where did it all go wrong? Buy this book and find out. Your ministry will never be the same again.

(c) Everyone else. Amateur Christians, ordinary laity and gormless pew fillers. After all, with your secular jobs you're the ones who can afford to buy it. Consider this a way of giving much-needed financial support to the work of the Kingdom, to atone in part for your unspiritual, materialistic lifestyle.

I believe that this book will really speak into your situation, and you will be enriched by it in a very real way. I hope to be enriched by it myself in an even more real way.

I would be reluctant to set myself up as a master pastor to instruct, exhort and chastise all who lead and feed the flocks of the Almighty, as I am not worthy for such a task – but then that's just the kind of humility that proves I am worthy after all. I really feel the Lord just telling me that, lo, here I am, willing to serve the shepherds of his vineyards. But let not the glory go unto me who am but a Kinder Egg for the gifts of the Lord.

'But who exactly is Rev. Gerald Ambulance?' you may ask (if you've been living under a bushel for the last ten years).

I am minister of the famous, some would say infamous (but it's not, it's just famous) St Ursula's High Pentecostal-

Reformed Church in Lewisham. Many know me better as a hard-hitting but entertaining preacher at the annual Exegesis for the Common Man festival, whose appropriate illustrations make you laugh and think, unlike some I could mention.

You might also know me as the writer of such anointed worship songs as 'O God You're Really Lord', 'Tell Me the Good Old Story (About Who's Not Going to Glory)', and the young people's favourite 'I Wanna Be a Jehovah Pavlova (The Justified Desserts Song)'.

Others will know me as the writer of countless soul-saving tracts like *Will You Be Sky-Walking when Jesus Strikes Back?*, *How to Avoid Eye Contact During the Grace*, and *Demons Knifing Your Eyeballs and Boiling Your Groin for All Eternity, or Sunday Morning at Your Local High Pentecostal-Reformed Church? The Choice Is Yours*.

Still others will know me for my 'with-it' modern problem ministry bringing words of guidance, encouragement and chastisement as the agony priest of such quasi-Christian publications and websites as *disclosure* and Ship of Fools.

You might also know me as archsteward of RGA Ministries, equipping the people of God with everything needful for the spiritual life, from Holy Martyrs Burn Again Candles to the Leviticus Theme Park.

Most of you will know me as all of them. So let me lead you down these paths of anointed ministry that none knows so well as I. And as we walk, may the dove of anointment rest on thy head and deposit a rich blessing.

I must also acknowledge everyone who has made this great work possible. (I do apologize but it's in the contract.) First of all, Him before Whom we are all but as the gone-off cucumber of time in the salad tray of eternity (God), closely followed by me. A long way behind in third place are Sibling Darren and those well-meaning quasi-Christians at *disclosure* who have published my humble words for years at great peril to their souls and pockets and have given me permission to repeat stuff I may inadvertently have said before, in return for a Get Out Of Purgatory Free Card.

Sibling Simon of the Ship of Fools has also stored up for himself considerable treasure in heaven (no cash alternative) for his help to the work of the Lord through me. Then there are my dear disturbed online flock at Ship of Fools and my *disclosure* readers, for being so forthcoming with such fruitful and entertaining problems. And lastly the beloved sister who in her holy humility has pleaded that her name be in no way connected with this mighty work. May thou have the feet of an athlete in thy pursuit of good purpose, without the associated fungal infections.

In the fleecing of the lambs of the Lord
Rev. Gerald Ambulance
St Homobonus of Cremona's Day, 2001

Note: For that extra reality factor, I have concluded each chapter with real-life problems brought unto me by genuine punters on problem pages, pastoral visits, counselling, confession, etc. I am sure they would be glad to know that their difficulties and weaknesses are being transformed from a sordid secret into a great blessing and encouragement for many, pointing the way in the darkness, or at least making us all realize we're not so bad after all. Amen?

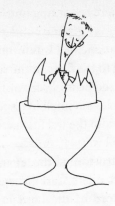

How I got started

Let me start with the inspirational story of how the Lord raised me from the humble depths of ordinary Christianity to the even humbler heights of anointed ministry.

I was born to God-fearing parents (they were also frightened of ghosts and hamsters), and brought up in the church, though I was allowed home on Saturdays. I went through a short rebellious phase as a teenager, losing concentration during the 27th verse of 'O God That Smote in Days of Yore'. I was finally won for the Lord by an open-air evangelist yelling 'Repent! The end of the world is nigh' – though I later realized he was exaggerating.

It was in my late teens that I first heard, clear as the crystal sea, the call unto ministry. It was after the youth club disco, which I had been sitting outside for three hours (partly on conscientious grounds and partly because the only time I ever tried dancing I was leapt on by the St John Ambulance and held to the floor in the recovery position), experimenting with the possibilities of transubstantiating snakebite. And behold an infallibly spooky voice spake unto me, saying, 'Go into the world, Rev. Gerald, and reach out to them with my love.'

I followed this instruction to the letter, and ended up in Peckham Juvenile Offenders' Care Centre. And while I was there, behold, the word of the Lord came to me again, saying, 'OK, I can see I'm going to have to be a little more literal. I forgot you were a fundamentalist. How about "Preach the gospel"?' So this was the path I followed, in a part-time, amateur, non-famous way, for years.

I felt the call to serve the Lord full-time about the same time as I was sacked from the Department of Social Security for laying hands on the unemployed. I enrolled at the Bangor Indoctrination Institute on the BJ course, but in my first term there I was forced to reprimand them for being unable to tell me anything I didn't already know from reading the Bible.

So in the vacation they all went away and found out background information and scholarly opinions, which they came back and taught us in the spring term. I was then forced to denounce them all as notorious heretics for teaching us things that weren't in the Bible. Pausing only to call down fire from heaven upon that forsaken pit of desolation, I returned home and developed my tract-writing ministry.

My first anointed outpouring, *So You Don't Think Ezekiel Was a Pre-Tribulationist?*, now universally recognized as being a bit heavy going, was not the worldshaking blockbuster you would expect if you are familiar with my later work. But I learned a lot from the experience.

Then, while on my annual furlough in Aberdeen, enjoying the beauty of God's great earth and blessing some of the local wildlife with my barbecuing ministry, I came across a copy of a programme for a local amateur dramatic society's production of *Jaws*. And on p. 11, under an advert for Ewan McSpewan's, 'Brewed in a ditch for the lagerist with discernment', I saw this:

ST URSULA'S HIGH PENTECOSTAL-REFORMED CHURCH, LEWISHAM

We are looking to appoint a new youth elder, to replace Brother Alan Mullarkey who has passed on after 47 years' faithful service.

You can imagine how excited I was to find a church with such confidence in the Lord that they advertised a post 500 miles away where no applicants would ever read it apart from the one man miraculously selected by God. And that man was me. I immediately packed away my tent, shotgun and barbecue and took a one-way journey to Lewisham.

I found the church, with a bearded man putting up a poster of a yellow young man saying, 'Don't have a cow, man, have faith in the Lord Jesus.'

I cried, 'It is I, the one predestined from before all time to take up the post of youth elder at St Ursula's High Pentecostal-Reformed Church!'

He said, 'Pleased to meet you. I'm the new youth elder of St Ursula's High Pentecostal-Reformed Church.'

They'd employed the wrong person! Tricky situation. What was I to do?

We brought the burden before the body – and before the throne, it goes without saying – with prayer, fasting and a real sense of prostration and impalement. We ascertained that it was God's will for the two rivals for the post to go outside for a memory-verse shoot-out, members of the congregation calling out book, chapter and verse, the true youth elder of the church being decided by who was first to recite the verse correctly.

You will not be surprised to hear that the best man won (me), even though my specialist subject (Levitical abominations) didn't come up once. I thrashed him (immediately after winning the contest) and cast him forth into outer darkness, from where it is just a short walk to the bus station.

It was in this post that I developed my worship, preaching and tract-writing ministries. All that remained was for the Lord to raise me up to be minister of St Ursula's, which he did when Rev. Enoch passed sadly away in a freak eucharistic mishap. (Whatever rumours you may have heard in the non-Christian press and on certain scandal-loving Channel 4 programmes, he was accidentally transubstantiated as he presided, and had to eat himself.)

How to pastor

Some people imagine that a minister only has to work on Sunday! I know I did when I took on the job, but nothing could be further than the truth. When I'm not performing, I'm pastoring: leading my flock down the path of righteousness, the road of encouragement and the motorway of triumphalness – all at once!

Prayer

A typical day – if there is such a thing for a famous spiritual giant – starts early with my gruelling regime of prayer. Prostrate in intercession, meditation and prophetic visions, I am often taken right out of the earthly realm.

This work is so important for the church and for the day ahead, I don't even raise my head from under the duvet till I've put in a good couple of hours.

Outdoor ministry

Every day, I walk the streets of Lewisham, blessing everywhere I go. I give particularly prayerful attention to the houses of the faithful, of course, and sometimes nip round to the back windows for a pastoral check-up on the spiritual correctfulness of their homelife. I bring my Super-Spirt-U-All Holy Water Pistol (£29.99 from RGA Ministries) to deliver an extra anointing on local doorsteps. I used to sprinkle them with sacred oil, but after local enemies of the Way got together to sue St Ursula's for several million pounds in damages for injuries and greasy post, I felt led to change tactics.

I also make a point of visiting centres of spiritual oppression in the area. One day, I might be casting out territorial spirits from the Crown Inn under the cover of having a turkey sandwich and lemonade. Another, I'm breaking the godless windows of Lewisham Methodist and draping their railings with cassette tape of the Tim Splendid Worship Trio. Another day, I'm laying saintly hands of deliverance on the pages of various worldly magazines in the corner shop, until Mr Saddeque starts getting shirty – which is typical of the kind of opposition you have to expect if you're about this kind of work. It just proves how worried the Enemy is.

On Mondays, I incorporate a trip to the bank to pay in Sunday's offering. Unfortunately there is almost always someone begging outside. I don't like to give them money, because it just encourages them to live off other people. But I have something far more valuable – a prayer. And a tract called *No Home? No Hope? Go to Church.*

Then there are the occasional extras: addressing the Parents/Guardians and Toddlers group; ecumenical discussion with the Medium-Low Pentecostal-Reformed Church; popping into the Senior Citizens' Volleyball club for first aid and last rites. This week, for example, I was on assembly duty at Avalon Gardens Primary School. According to the rota I was supposed to tell them about Daniel in the lion's den, but I felt really convicted to share with them my recent highly acclaimed sermon on the curses of Jeremiah. By the time I'd got to 'H is for Heart (and the hardness thereof)', the entire reception class had wet themselves and I had to go and change my shoes. This really is frontline spiritual warfare.

Flock problems

As the great Nathaniel Egbiter said, in his unauthorized autobiography, *God's Loony*, 'A church with no congregation needs no minister.' Which is a shame, because the job would be a lot more edifying without them.

Much of my time is given to pastoral visits, either to the ill and infirm to rebuke them for not having the faith to claim their healing, or to problem members to listen to their whinging and blubbing and put them right. I care more deeply than you can imagine for even the most trivial, ludicrous and boring problems that my followers come up with, but you really wouldn't believe the kind of flock you get these days. Still, sign of the times, I suppose. The important thing is that I bring a little light into the darkness of these wayward so-called Christians – though, now I think about it, not as much as the darkness they bring into mine. Still, the job has to be done.

Here are the twelve most popular questions I've come across in the pastoral ministry, and the right answers.

Problem 1: I'm feeling depressed.

Answer: Nonsense! How can a Christian be depressed when God has filled the world with lovely things like redemption and theology and little baby birds? You must be totally ungrateful and a very bad Christian. Try counting your blessings. When I need cheering up I just count other people's blessings, but then I'm probably rather more spiritual than you. Anyway, it will all be all right when you're dead.

Problem 2: I have a really big problem, but it's just too embarrassing for me to say what it is.

Answer: Come now, there's no need to feel burdened. All Christians have problems, however saved they are. Even I am sometimes tempted to be more humble than I ought. Remember, a problem shared is a new sermon illustration. My advice is to leave it all at the foot of the cross, if you can find one, and feel OK.

Problem 3: I'm confused about the Trinity. How can God and Jesus and the Holy Spirit all be God, if there's only one God?

Answer: Look at it like this: once upon a time there were three little bunnies called Flopsy, Mopsy and Cottontail. One day a nasty man caught them and put them in a rabbit pie. They were still three rabbits, but only one pie. (Although the pie got cut into lots of pieces, admittedly.) To put it in plain language that even a complete dur-brain could understand, the three persons of the triune Godhead are one in substance, but in three hypostases. If you have any further questions, don't hesitate to ask someone else.

Problem 4: My dog just died. Will he be in heaven?
Answer: Not if I have anything to do with it, he won't. Can't stand the nasty, smelly, woofy things. How could it be heaven with them barking all the time and leaving their little chocolate parcels everywhere?

Problem 5: I have this really strong urge to put on my sister's dresses when she's out. Is this wrong?
Answer for a woman: You should really ask your sister first. If she says no, give her a copy of my reasonably priced booklet *Dare to Share Your Flares (and Other Items of Clothing) with Those Less Fortunate Than Yourself.*
Answer for a man: What do you want to wear dresses for? They're women's clothes, you know. If you haven't got any nice things of your own, try Oxfam, where you can get some natty shirts and tank tops very cheaply. If you can't help wearing frocks, I must lovingly and acceptingly say that you are disgusting and evil, and you should either kill yourself or become a priest so you can wear all the dresses you like.

Problem 6: Is it wrong for Christians to drink?
Answer: Not at all. Christians need to drink just like ordinary human beings. After all, the good Lord created our mouths and he created water, so why shouldn't we put the one into the other? (This rule doesn't apply to everything that God created, though.)

Problem 7: Er, yes. I was thinking more of alcoholic drinks, actually.

Answer: Alcohol! What can have put such unspiritual thoughts into your head? Alcohol is the outpouring of Beelzebub's bladder. Anything that makes people lose control, laugh, talk madly and fall over must be very very bad, unless it's the Holy Spirit, in which case it's very very good. Obviously, when Jesus told his disciples to drink wine in the Lord's Supper, he didn't mean it literally. He meant it as a deeply meaningful symbol, to symbolize non-alcoholic transubstantiated grape juice.

Problem 8: My friend Gordon is a Mormon. I know they're wrong and everything, but what exactly is it they believe?

Answer: You must have nothing more to do with this enemy of righteousness. Your eternal soul is in danger of pollution. Imagine if he made you doubt what you have been told, and see things from his point of view! I have no idea what these misled sinners believe, but since it's wrong, why would anyone want to find out?

Problem 9: I'm very sensitive about my huge horrible nose.

Answer: My word, it is a whopper, isn't it? I suggest you always turn to face people head on when you talk to them, so they don't see it in full shocking profile. Don't turn too fast, though. You could also try wearing a big funny hat to distract attention from it. Make sure it's very big and very funny, though. Alternatively, just remember that man (and woman these days!) looks at the outside, but God looks at the inside. This is good news for you as one of the few people whose insides look no worse than their outsides.

Problem 10: I find it hard to love God when I think

that he's going to send my friends to burn in hell. How can I get over this hurdle?

Answer: Simple. Just remember that if you don't, you'll be joining them.

Problem 11: Is there anything actually wrong with swearing? I know you shouldn't take the Lord's name in vain, but what about all the non-religious swear words that the Bible doesn't mention, like ****, ****, *******, etc?

Answer: OK, so the Bible doesn't explicitly say anything about this, but if you read between the lines it says it's a very bad sin – as long as you read between the right lines. St Paul's swearing at the Philippians was of course just an unfortunate lapse. After all, what would the world think of Christians if they said, 'Oh arse!' when things went wrong? Can you imagine Abraham saying 'Damn, my sandal's broken'?

Problem 12: I find church boring.

Answer: Well, it isn't. Church is always exciting and interesting, because it's all about God and redemption and intercession. I suggest you buy a copy of my tract *Condemning Words for Spiritual Failures*, and have a good think.

Problem flock

I'm happy to say my followers at St Ursula's have always been perfectly united in their devotion and submission to their humble servant and divine stand-in, me. But, alas, there are often troublemakers among them who refuse to join in this unity, sometimes carrying the whole church along in their rebellion and heresy.

The Bible warns us that in these last days such dissenters will come, deceiving even the elect if it were possible – and the bad news is it's a piece of cake. In the good old days, you could have had them smoking on a stick for such apostasy, but in these godless times you can't hit a sulky Sunday schooler about the head with a stole without getting into trouble with the local authorities.

So, how to keep your flock on the rails:

Lateness

Being late for church dishonours God and man. (And woman these days!) After all, I have to get there half an hour early. And God has been there from all eternity, so is it so much to ask?

In St U's, for each minute that each individual is late, I extend my sermon for a minute. Last Sunday, for example, a family of four, five minutes late, allowed me to get from Jeremiah to Amos in my 'Survey of Curses Against the Moabites' mini-series. The collective hostility of the fellowship towards the offenders means that they rarely re-offend, or indeed return. And good riddance.

Purgatory

I keep a set of thermometers at the back of the church measuring how much roasting time in Purgatory each member has banked for their miserable offences. This is simple to do – you just need an Iniquity Slide Rule (£39.99 from RGA Ministries) to work out the scale. The slide rule will also tell you what penances to give, from your basic ten Abba Fathers and ten Shine Jesus Shines right up to a pilgrimage to Toronto barefoot and with water wings.

False teaching

Practically everything is false teaching if you look into it enough, so you have to choose your battleground. In fact the only people who don't seem to have succumbed to wilful ignorance of the truth are God and me. (And in fact even I used to be wrong about a few things.) Thank goodness we two at least can see eye to eye.

* * *

The Rev. Testifies

Sibling Bill Sweetie, a beloved bro. but a bit of a pain in the Balaam's ass, once preached a sermon on Eutychus falling out of the upstairs window, which he claimed was 'an amazing miraculous prediction of Chris Eubank being ejected from the *Celebrity Big Brother* house'.

I gently corrected him, explaining, 'You distort the plain meaning of the gospel with your godless imaginings, thou unclean heretic! It is clear to any that have eyes to see that this passage is about Vanessa Feltz being ejected from the *Celebrity Big Brother* house.'

The argument continued for a number of hours until all the congregation had left, and, alas, he himself went without being reconciled to the truth. So the following week I introduced a new chorus:

The Lord loves us all, the Lord loves us all,
Whether we're big or whether we're small
Whether we're sexy as Warren Beatty
Or fat, thick and sinful as Sibling Sweetie.

Bill stood and shouted, 'Who are you calling fat? You can't say that in a hymn!'

'Sorry', I explained, 'there's nothing I can do about it, it's from the Lord. Besides, you're the only one who rhymes with Beatty.'

His heart was hardened, and he ran from the church, yelling, 'Well, the Lord's told me to slay you, you unclean Amalekite, and we're not talking slain in the Spirit.'

I let Bill sleep on it for a few hours, and then climbed through his bedroom window wearing my alb of discipline. But he awoke, and said, 'Gabriel? What is it this time?'

Evidently he didn't have his contacts in, and before I had a chance to correct his misapprehension I had spoken forth unto him in a deep booming voice, saying, 'You told Rev. Gerald Ambulance that the Lord had told you to slay him.'

'He did tell me to slay him.'

'You misheard, Bill. The Lord actually told you to flay him. No, hang on – pray for him, that was it. Yes, pray for him.'

And from that moment Sibling Bill was once again walking in the light. Another success story for the Lord!

* * *

Excommunication

We have a special ministry for persistent offenders of the Lord at St Ursula's. The deacons take them out the back and excommunicate them. With baseball bats.

Of course, extending the middle finger of fellowship is

never final. I make it clear to these lost sheep that the doors are always open (however heavily guarded), and advise them to examine their consciences – preferably in a moment of vulnerability and self-loathing – and then come crawling back for forgiveness. If the Lord is willing, I re-admit them to our little flock, after they've completed a two-year course of penance and re-education. I call it the Beta course.

* * *

The Rev. Testifies

Our sibling Maureen Spenk would not give over her wrongful belief that the third goat in the book of Daniel represented Belgium. (Or was it that it didn't represent Belgium? Anyway, whichever interpretation is completely alien to the plain meaning of the Scriptures. It was a long time ago now.) I reasoned with her, chastised her, even devoted a term's house-group programme to the subject (which she perversely refused to attend).

I excommunicated her repeatedly, but she just kept coming. She secretly sneaked in and replaced our Impaling of St Bernard banner with a Belgian flag depicting a goat eating chips and mayonnaise. So in the end I had a word in the appropriate quarters and had her prematurely raptured.

* * *

The last resort

Now, you might have heard all kinds of hysterical hyped-up stories in the press about St Ursula's stoning blasphemers and burning heretics. Rest assured, the death penalty is entirely biblical. For which is worse, a short sharp shock that might make someone see sense at the last minute, or eternal burning? Enemies of the Way love to whinge about human rights, but how much good will rights do them when they're sinking in the lake of fire and wailing into the starless night, 'If only I had forsaken my misguided ways and followed Rev. Gerald Ambulance in the paths of correctfulness while there was still time'? Not much, that's how much.

Ask the Rev.

I am a fellow suckler of the lambs of Zion, being Chief Priest at The Congregation of Neo-Apostolic Joy and Infinite Sobriety in Greenwich. When I go away on retreats, missions and crusades, they change the locks, bar the windows and pretend not to be there when I come back. How should I deal with them?

REV. LEONARD K. MEMBRANE

The Rev. says:
Canons, Sibling Rev., it's the only language they understand. Blow the doors down and run in howling curses from the Old Testament. Then throw them all out insisting that if they want to come back they have to start again from the beginning and go through five years of Sunday school before they're allowed into the church. That's what I did when my congregation tried to take over the church, and I'm glad to say that most of those wicked worldlings were so ashamed of their folly they never came back.

May I take a moment of your valuable time to let you know how blessed I have been by my Super-Spirt-U-All

Holy Water Pistol. It has brought a whole new dimension to my spiritual outlook and made me more confident and respected as a minister.

[The next bit's a little heretical so I'll tactfully skip it.]

Beatitudinous outpourings upon you.

JOHN PAUL II

PS I'm not really sure about your taking over here when I 'answer the glorious homecoming call', to be honest. I don't have that much say in it, and then there's the whole 'separated brother' thing. Still, I'll see what I can do.

JPII

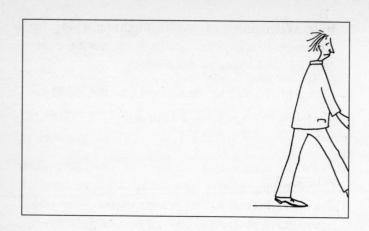

How to motivate/demotivate

It would be an understatement of apocalyptic proportions to say that many members of my church are half-hearted about their faith. A lot are only quarter-hearted and I could name a few who would be hard-pressed to come up with one left ventricle between them. They evidently believe they pay me to do their religion for them. I've checked my contract, and actually they're right, but I'm not going to tell them that.

Here are some congregational motivation strategies for you:

Encouragement

Being nice, basically. It doesn't work.

'The little you do for the church is much appreciated,' you say. 'How lovely it would be to see you taking on more.'

'Thanks, Father,' they say. 'See you next week. Oh no, I'm going to a boot sale. Well, whenever.'

Challenging

This doesn't work either.

'We desperately need someone to do Peals on Wheels now that Sibling Eileen's car has passed on,' you announce to the congregation. 'If no one comes forward, then this fruitful door-to-door bell-ringing ministry will have to stop. There are many of you who just aren't doing enough for the Lord. Come on, siblings, let's see some of you really making that step of responsefulness.'

So, immediately after the service the three people who already between them keep just about every meeting, committee and project in the church going come up to me with haggard, haunted expressions and say, 'I think I could fit it in on alternate Thursday nights between knitting for missionaries and the swimming in the Spirit workshop.' There comes a point where even a minister has to say 'don't worry'.

Rebuking

Hammering the pulpit and gesticulating prophetically, you cry, 'You are a sorry excuse for Christians. After all the Lord has done for you – everything, really – still none of you is willing to run the young offenders' group. You are ungrateful, impious, sluggish, worldly, false-hearted, rebellious, faithless, two-timers of the Almighty. A stench in the divine nostril.'

This doesn't work either. They just stare blankly back, as if to say, 'We know, you tell us every week' – apart from the ones who are looking round the rest of the church smugly, thinking, 'I hope they're taking this in.'

Other measures

They don't work either.

If you can't beat 'em

After years of encouragement, challenges, rebukes and physical threats failed to overcome their apathy, I decided to try a different approach: give up. After all, why should I bother if they don't?

If you too would like to try a Service of Non-Committal, here is the outline for mine:

> Opening mumble
> 250 'Crown Him with Several Crowns'
> Reading: Pizza delivery menu (Sponsored by Catford Pizza Palais)
> 157 'Jesus We Celebrate Your Nil–Nil Draw'
> 83 'Lord I Lift Your Name Up a Bit'
> Prayer for the lost:
> – the keys to the music cupboard;
> – Sibling Derek's lottery ticket;
> – Sibling Susan's sister's marbles.
> Liturgical spot:
> *Minister:* Let us confess our sins to the Lord.
> *People:* Let's not.

Open worship: (Max two from the following)
'Show Your Towel, O Lord'
'The Price is Deferred (Nothing to Pay till 2004!)'
'Be Still or You'll Wake Up Mrs Brooks'
'From Devon You Came'
'Brian Blessed be the Name of the Lord'
'Come On and Sellotape'
'There is Power in the Name of Jeff Powers'
'We are More Than Conkers'

Sermon: 'Two Steps to Faster Praying'
157 'When Yawning Gilds the Skies'
Eucharist take-out

Unfortunately no one actually turned up to the service, and the whole thing was abandoned. Fortunately this meant I could get home in time for *Coronation Street*.

Over-enthusiasm

At the same time as all this, you have people fervently and doggedly volunteering themselves for work in which they have absolutely no ability whatsoever. Now, in theory, a sense of calling and a heart for service are more important than such worldly concerns as 'quality' and 'success'. In practice, though, you have to snap them out of it before they turn your church into a museum of lameness. Be gentle but firm.

* * *

The Rev. Testifies

Sibling Bill Sweetie considers himself to have a song-writing ministry, and insists on coming round to play me his latest excrescences. His last one went something like this:

Hooray for Jesus! Let's all cheer it!
Hooray for Jesus! And the Holy Spirit!
Hooray for Jesus! Let him hear it!
I know he hears everything we say,
But it makes him happy when we shout hooray!

Only slightly worse.

'What do you think, Reverend?' he asked.

'Well, Bill,' I said, 'let me put it like this . . .' And I was about to break his ukulele over his head and make him eat the pieces, but when I saw him nodding and grinning like a big idiotic puppy, I was overcome by a spirit of tactfulness.

'I'm not saying it's a bad song,' I told him. 'It has its merits. It's just that all other songs I've heard so far in my life are better. A lot, lot better. And not just songs – the same goes for all sounds of any kind. I think I speak for the human race as a whole here, when I say we'd rather be surrounded for eternity by car alarms, screaming children and Hear'Say than ever have to listen to that song ever again.'

'You can't say that!' he cried. 'That song was given me by the Lord.'

'No, Bill, it was given to you by Satan for the demoralization and destruction of the church. It's about time you learnt to tell the difference. Now go home and develop a less stupid spirituality.

'Oh, and by the way,' I added as he was doing up his sandals. 'Just in case you were thinking of bringing it before the church in our open worship, let me direct you to the verse in Proverbs that says, "It is better to sing with contentment the songs of our fathers than to be impaled on the pole that Sibling Norman uses to open the high window." Now that, I think, is from the Lord.'

* * *

How to preach

A little girl in my church once had a rabbit that was very poorly. Unfortunately the local vet is not a believer, so the family had to put Hezekiah Bunny to sleep themselves. Mummy and Daddy just couldn't bring themselves to do it, so I had to come and take it away for a time of slaying.

And preaching is like that. Most people wouldn't want to do it, and no one wants it done to them, but it's for the best.

Personally, I know no deeper joy and blessing than mounting the pulpit to wield the sharp two-edged sword of the Word, and decapitating my congregation with it. How fast 40 minutes can fly when you're hammering home the truth about the personality problems of the judges under three points beginning with P!

Preaching is the absolute number one priority for the anointed servant of the Lord, along with the administration of the sacraments, the fullness of the gifts and the balancing of the books. And the wearing of the correct chasuble for the liturgical season, of course. You have a lot of priorities in this job – it just shows how important it is.

You yourselves have probably heard me expounding the word with power and authority at the Exegesis for the Common Man festival, or in High Pentecostal-Reformed churches up and down the country, or outside Lewisham Woolworth's with a megaphone, a trolley full of tracts and a catapult.

I first realized I had the gift of preaching one day when I suddenly found I had been talking to myself for half an hour. And as I listened, behold, the sound of my voice was so pleasing unto mine ear that I knew I could not keep it to myself, but must speak forth to bring truth into the darkness of men's hearts. (And women's these days!)

So if you would follow in my humble steps up the stairs to the main stage, here's how.

Preparing

This is important for the beginner, though the more you grow in maturity, the more you can rely on the prompting of the Spirit. I still have the last sermon notes I ever wrote:

Sunday evening, Third after Trinity, 1995

1   Open the Bible, and read a few chapters.
2   Glare at the congregation.
3   Wait for inspiration.

(If in doubt, go back to 1, and try again.)

Which text?

If your church has a lectionary, then finding your passage
is no problem. For those of us who prefer to get God's
word from God, though, there are various ways to hear his
prompting.

(a) Getting yourself into a spiritually receptive frame of
    mind, take the sacred Scriptures in your hand, and
    recite this prayer:
    Which all-hallowed text
    Should I preach on next?
    Then open a page at random and the first words you
    see will be the Lord's chosen passage for you. If you
    get the contents page, or one of those passages that
    sounds misleadingly like heresy, you obviously
    weren't praying spiritually enough.

(b) If something especially interesting and amusing has
    happened to you recently, then you have yourself a
    sermon illustration. Think up a spiritual point it
    could illustrate, and then all you have to do is find a
    passage that says something similar.

(c) To save you and the Spirit the bother of going through
    all this every week, you can have a sermon series. Preach
    through a book of the Bible half a chapter a week till,
    nine months later, your flock have entered into a whole
    new level in their understanding and appreciation of it
    and never want to read it again. Or choose a theme that
    is close to your heart, and pick all the passages that will
    best back up what you want to say. For example, some of
    my series have included 'The Lord's Message to Tony
    Blair', 'Lesser Known Levitical Abominations', 'What the
    Scriptures Say about Teachers Not Clearing Up after

Sunday School', '12 Great Biblical Killings', 'The Lord's Message to Sibling Bill Sweetie', and 'Ch. 3 v. 16 in Every Book of the Bible (Except the Very Short Ones)'.

What to say

So you've got your text, what are you going to say about it? It depends what kind it is.

The obvious bits

If it's a straightforward passage that no one can misunderstand or disagree with, then – in theory – once you've read it, the congregation has learned everything it's going to learn and you might as well stop there. In practice, however, that means there'd be no sermon. So you need to fill out your time repeating it in different words, and telling stories that clarify the meaning. If it is not possible to make it any clearer than it already is, then tell stories that obscure the meaning, so you can then clarify it.

Greek is another good time-killer. Try this kind of thing:

'Now the word translated "preaching" here is the Greek word *kerygma*. And that comes from the verb *kerysso*, meaning "to preach". So when St Paul says "preaching", what that word really means is "preaching".'

Or alternatively:

'The word translated "Spirit" here is the Greek word *pneuma* which means "wind". And that's where we get the term "pneumatic tyres" from. So what St Paul really means when he says "Be filled with the Spirit" is that we should be like the tyres of the Lord, ready to go anywhere for him, adding comfort to his journey

through eternity and ever vigilant for the broken glass of
the Enemy. Or full of wind, alternatively.'

The dodgy bits

Some passages of the Bible seem to the unenlightened to
be theologically unsound. For example, despite the fact
that St Paul clearly says we are justified by faith alone,
others such as James, Jesus, Peter and Paul, as well as the
Old Testament writers, often seem to suggest the most
important thing is what we do.

The principle here is to interpret such obscure texts in
the light of the clear ones. If a verse says something you
can't accept, it can't really mean it, so find one you do
accept, and explain that since the Bible can't contradict
itself, they must both mean the same.

The boring bits

Some people are unspiritual enough to find a page full of
various chaps begetting each other, or census returns of
the tribes of Israel, a tad uninspiring. Should you, for the
sake of our weaker members, avoid such stuff in your
sermons? Certainly not. God put these bits in the Bible for
a good reason, whatever it might be. It's probably his way
of saying it's a sin to take things too easy.

Boredom is just a part of being a Christian, I'm afraid.
If all the people who fell asleep in my sermons were laid
end to end, they'd be a lot more comfortable – but it's
not going to happen. That's why I appointed Sibling
Norman Sandal as deacon with a long stick and a
prodding ministry.

The unbelievable bits

Did God really create the world in six days? Did Joshua make the sun stand still? Was the bread in the Last Supper really Jesus' body? Is the Lord really a shepherd?

Most scholars and preachers these days have come to see that some bits of the Bible are more factual than others. They are very bad men. If they tried that in my pulpit, I'd show them what a 'two-edged sword piercing even to the dividing asunder of joints and marrow' is literally like. May the locusts of Moab devour their progeny, the false sons of perdition! There's no such thing as unbelievable, only unbelievers.

You must teach that everything in the Bible is factual, exact and unerring, as it clearly says in the Bible somewhere. Towards the back of one of those long books, I think.

If a single statement of the Bible were wrong then the whole thing would be worthless, just as if anything ever said by a preacher was wrong then preaching would be worthless. Thank the Lord that's never happened.

If you can't help feeling that a particular passage goes against all sense and reason, then abandon sense and reason. If you still can't believe it, just pretend you can so you don't worry the flock.

How long?

A recent survey from the Bureau of Depressing Religious Statistics says this:

> The average churchgoer remembers 0.03 per cent of all sermons heard.

After 10 minutes, he (or she these days!) starts thinking about lunch.

After 20 minutes, they stop hearing a word you say and start finding the notice sheet interesting. (At least you've worked one miracle.)

After 30 minutes, they've forgotten the bit they actually listened to at the beginning.

After 40 minutes, they start wondering if it's possible to commit suicide by impaling themselves on their car keys.

How should we respond to such surveys? Burn them. And their compilers where available. It's just ammunition for those who would do down the holy art of the sermon – those who want to fastforward to the bit where they can get sacramental or charismatic or both depending on their bent. If they don't feel they're getting much out of your sermons, preach a series on 'Sermons: God's Number One Priority', and hopefully they'll see the error of their ways.

Some say it's impossible these days to hold people's attention for a half-hour monologue. But they forget that the most popular stand-up comedians manage it – despite being profane and worldly – with material they've worked on for two months. So why shouldn't most preachers manage it with a few hours' prep on Saturday afternoon and the miraculous empowerment of Almighty God? After all, which is more truly interesting, the eternal mysteries of salvation, or some pointless rubbish about whether you've ever noticed that when you're in a queue at the supermarket the other one always goes quicker? I rest my case. (The answer is 'the eternal mysteries of salvation'.)

Thus saith the Lord

* * *

The Rev. Testifies

I once had a student preacher, whom we'll call Dan to protect his real identity. 'Dan' had the bad habit of saying, 'That's what I think,' or 'This is just my opinion' when he was preaching.

'That's no good, Colin,' said the congregation, 'we want to know what God says.'

Then one day he said, 'I believe the time is come to consider with a very real sense of prostration and flagellation those truths which have been graciously vouchsafed unto us. But I could be wrong.' So they took him out into the car park and stoned him, which was tough but fair: he'd admitted that he might be preaching falsehood. The Scriptures say we must stone a false prophet, but they don't say anything about not stoning a true prophet, so better to be on the safe side.

* * *

True preachers are but tannoys for the word of the Lord, and should have no opinions or personality of their own. Most find the second easier than the first. We who serve in the pulpit are mere empty vessels, irrelevant conduits to pipe the Word of Truth into the even more irrelevant receptacles sitting in the pews.

(Which, incidentally, means that certain worryingly popular so-called preachers I could mention, who got bigger crowds than me at this year's Exegesis for the Common Man, were evidently diluting the word of the Lord with their own observations, interpretations and anecdotes and therefore should never be asked back.)

You must make it clear that what you preach is the pure truth of God. Unfortunately preachers in churches across the world make the same claim while they loudly and emphatically contradict each other, so that means you have to say it louder and more emphatically than any of them.

Sometimes you will find what you have been preaching loudly and emphatically as the truth of God is in fact a dangerous heresy. Don't make a fuss, it only upsets people. Just start preaching the real truth, louder and more emphatically than ever to make up for lost time.

Ask the Rev.

I really try to believe everything in the Bible, but I don't know if I can now. The preacher on Sunday did a whole sermon on 'the fruits of the Spirit' – love, joy, peace, patience, kindness, etc. Well, excuse me, but am I the only one who's noticed? None of these are fruit! Is the Bible wrong? I'm relying on your wondrous powers of exegesis to save my faith.

KAREN MUESLI

The Rev. says:

It's a toughie, Karen, but I have sought the Lord, and he hath answered unto me. For behold, do not we all have two names, a Christian name and also a surname (some more sensible than others)? Well, these names you listed from the Bible are all the Christian names that God has given unto the fruit. Joy, for example, is the lemon's first name. Then you've got Patience Plum, Kindness Mango and Self-Control Tomato (which is a fruit, actually, though many people think it's only a veg).

Are you really sure about what you said on Sunday, that we must be willing to sacrifice to God whatever we most love in this world? Because I love jogging, but I just don't see how I can put it on an altar and burn it as a pleasing aroma unto the Lord.

SIBLING MANDY SLACK

The Rev. says:
You see, Sibling Mandy, this is one of several differences between me and God. When God says something, he has to express himself plainly and use every word literally so as not to confuse fundamentalists. I, however, am allowed to use figures of speech.

How to lead services

This isn't an issue if your church has liturgy instead of the Holy Spirit. The only thing you have to think about is half a dozen hymn numbers and whether your maniple is on straight. Unfortunately, liturgy is an abomination unto the Lord. I mean, how would you like to be worshipped in 500-year-old poetry instead of people making their own prayers up as they go along?

True worship – as opposed to the fossilized kind – sparkles in Spirit-filled spontaneity. It's saying what you want when you want (by which, of course, I mean what He wants when He wants), wild, free and unpredictable. The fact that it lasts exactly an hour and a half every week just shows that the Lord is in it. He likes order, you see, just not preparation.

I must admit that I like to use the creeds (with some minor adjustments of my own). This crowd of benighted Amalekites need to remind themselves what Christianity is on a weekly basis. As for reciting the confession, though, it's a nice idea, but it doesn't go into much detail, does it? I like to go round one by one and give everyone the chance to get their own specific trespasses off their chests and into the open. It really does help.

Lay interference

It is the policy at St Ursula's that the laity should be as involved in the service as possible – their policy, not mine, I hardly need add. It started innocently enough when I began letting them applaud sermons and do the actions to 'O for a Thousand Tongues'. Before I knew where I was, they're praying, heckling, prophesying, doing unscheduled readings from Song of Songs and lighting homemade incense.

They tell me how important it is for everyone in the church to lead everyone else, irrespective of status, coherence, orthodoxy or being one epistle short of a testament. Well, what would I know? I'm only the minister. Anyhow, I've managed to cut it down to a 15-minute spree supervised by Sibling Norman with a stopwatch and tear gas.

Language

To add that extra degree of sacred mystery to your worship, you can't beat doing it in Latin. If there's one thing better than worshipping in a language that's foreign to your congregation, it's doing it in a language that's foreign to everyone on the planet. So we have a Latin Mass once a week, a monthly Eucharist in Slavonic, and an annual communion service in tongues.

Worship

There are so many churches with so many different ways of worshipping God all claiming that theirs is the one style that God really likes. If only they could abandon this bigotry, forget their differences, realize that none of them is the 'one true way' and all join together in real High Pentecostal-Reformed worship. Now that *is* the one true way.

For who else treads the truly anointed path which unites the Spirit and the Rite, combining high-church flamboyance with high-on-the-Spirit antics? O, that all those who kiss the sacred page would also raise holy hands in liturgical ecstasy! That those who roll their eyes in prophetic abandon might stagger also under the influence of the incense! Let those who kneel to the Blessed Virgin keel also over under the touch. And let those who exorcise their household pets do so in the right tunicle for that date.

O ye dispersèd congregations of the lost sheep of the house of Zion! Will ye not turn again and come together to be united as one in these two equally important sides of the coin of sacred silliness? Let camp charismania flow like a burning mountain across this land.

Songs

It is good, where possible, to pick songs which reflect the theme of your sermon, so if half an hour is not enough for them to get what you're on about, all is not lost. However, while this is easy enough if you are preaching on how wonderful God is, it gets harder if there is much theological content in your word. It is possible, though, if you are creative. I managed to find songs for every one of my recent series 'Abominations of the Modern World' from insurance companies to climate change, and from co-habiting to stalking. ('Blessed Assurance', 'O Lord the Clouds are Gathering', 'Abide with Me' and 'O Love That Wilt Not Let Me Go' respectively).

I'm a great believer in repeating songs. When you think about it, the punters are either getting down and giving it all they've got, in which case let's milk it, or they're not, in which case you need to keep going till they do. I once had my lot singing the first line of 'God is Good' 311 times, trying to get them to *really* mean it, till the point when they were crying, going down in the Spirit, and hitting themselves over the head with *Hymns for Yesterday's Church* in their ecstasy. And I won't tell you how many times I had them singing 'Creator of the Rolling Spheres, Ineffably Sublime'.

Another thing. May I discourage everyone from saying to the worship leader 'Wow! I was thinking about "Hallelujah, I'm Feeling Peculiar" just before you announced it. It must really have been from the Lord.' For one thing, they're all from the Lord; and for another, what kind of confidence in the leader does it show if the Lord has to copy instructions to the congregation?

Eucharist

Our Lord turned water into wine, and we his earthly stand-ins turn wine into blood. It doesn't go down so well at parties, but it shows that wine-related miracles are at the heart of Christianity.

It doesn't get any better than this, dressed in my rainbow chasuble and fruits of the Spirit stole (made by the dear ladies of the Clergy Appreciation Group out of left-over banners), embroiled in clouds of incense and standing at the altar performing the impossible with the entire congregation out of sight.

Many centuries ago, the Church had the idea of replacing the bread with soluble polystyrene coins. Some churches have gone back to actual bread, but these are the same ones who replace the wine with non-alcoholic grape juice. Only St Ursula's combines the best of both worlds: coins and juice, for minimum crumbling and ecclesiastical inebriation. It also discourages those in the church tempted to take eucharistic terms like 'meal' and 'celebrate' too seriously.

Incense

Why is it that in this country fewer people are leaving Anglo-Catholic churches than any other? One answer might be that there were fewer there to start with, but there's more to it than that: incense addiction. Once that intoxicating holy smoke gets into their system, they'll never want to be without it. You can't beat Ol' Romanian, available from RGA Ministries (£19.99 for a 2oz baggy). This is top-grade stuff, powerful enough to be used for evangelistic purposes. Verily it gives a whole new meaning to 'high church'.

Alternative worship

A bizarre concept, considering how many alternative ways of worship there already are in the world. It always sounded dodgy to me, but Sibling Dave Wibblethorpe was always very keen on it, so I let him take a service. If it is something you feel the need to get out of your system, let me see what I can remember.

You turn off all the lights, light more nightlights than the human mind can comfortably conceive of, and put on a CD called something like *The Floaty Sounds of Clive Moon*. You then divide the room into the following zones:

Create

Put out a tray of Plasticine, pipe cleaners, milk-bottle tops and pairs of toy animals, so people can express their worship by recreating their favourite Bible stories.

Explore

Put up sheets of wallpaper and crayons so they can explore in words and pictures where they are really at and how they feel. Expect lots of 'Fine, thanks', 'Mustn't grumble', and 'I bless God for the tribulations that strengthen my perseverance and I'd love some more'.

Reflect

Set up a big mirror, and put up a Post-It note saying, 'All flesh shall wither and the beauty/ugliness thereof shall pass – Isaiah'. And another saying 'You look wonderful tonight – Eric Clapton'. Hang around next to it asking people if they see what you were getting at.

Focus

Set a slide projector to automatically show a series of snaps utterly unrelated to each other or anything else. I suggested to Sibling Dave that my holiday slides of the Holy Land would have been better, especially as I could have talked the congregation through them, reminding them of related Bible stories and eschatological prophecies. He just started muttering about 'the whole point', and 'escaping prescriptive paradigms', and 'overarching narratives'. Some people just lose themselves in jargon, don't they?

Embrace

I can't in good conscience describe this one. Standards are slipping enough already in church without encouraging this sort of behaviour.

Exegesis

This was my idea. You arrange some lovely flowers for people to sit and look at while they listen to a compilation tape of extracts from your greatest sermons, before getting distracted by the more trivial exhibits.

Challenge

Set out some pentagrams, goats' heads, virgins, etc., and invite worshippers to explore the liturgical traditions of Satanism. Put up a banner saying, 'Is your God big enough to take it?'

Encounter

This is what you and I would call a tea trolley. You just fill it with stuff to eat and drink, and people stand round it snacking and nattering and laughing and discussing the show. Alternative worship? An alternative to worship, more like.

Ask the Rev.

I have to lead a service in church and I'm going to introduce a whole lot of cool sounds from bhangra to punk folk. But I also want to keep the old people happy, so can you tell me the longest hymn in the whole world?

NAT STRUMMER

The Rev. says:
The answer is 'O Sacred Branch' by Capt. Habakkuk Bauldie. It starts:

When Adam, unclothed patriarch,
God's dictum followeth,
His holy seed bestowed on Eve,
From thence begat he Seth.

O Sacred Branch! O Root Divine!
O Blessèd Hebrew Family Tree!
With joy sublime we trace thy line,
Thou Script'ral genealogy.

It basically traces the Israelite family tree for just over a thousand verses from the start of the Old Testament through to Bob Dylan. It originated in America, where it is now illegal in some states for health and safety reasons. I think it's quite good, though.

How to do youth work

I fervently believe that today's young people are the Church of tomorrow, and it is the most depressing fact I can think of. It is an area I have had plenty of experience in, mostly bad, as I was youth elder of St Ursula's for a long stretch before becoming the minister. I will share with you what I can, but I've done my best to forget about it.

It is so important to meet young people where they're at if at all possible (except that they're usually in the grave-yard drinking cider in my experience). I forced myself to wear a back-to-front baseball cap, watch the less offensive moments of *Top of the Pops* and say 'Cool' whenever possible, in order to reach out to the youth of the church. And the Lord was with me all the way (as he had been with me all the time till then, and with everyone else too, in a very real sense).

To expand the work, I went out to the Lewisham street gangs devoted to vandalism, shouty music and under-age smoking, coming among them as one of their own. After a narrow escape with the police, I invited them to come along on a Friday night for the Scriptural Youngsters' Society, tuck shop and non-competitive table tennis. To my lasting joy, praisefulness and deep blessing they said no. (Or words to that effect.)

So I turned to a safer way to claim the blessing of growth – leaflet-bombing other church youth groups to draw in their members – and the Lord gave me great fruit. The secret of youth publicity is to use their stunted attention span to your advantage. Thus:

4 May   THE NEW MADONNA VIDEO Watch Sister Agatha Stoop's fascinating introduction to veneration of the Blessed Virgin.

11 May   McDONALD'S TRIP Interesting and thought provoking slides from Sibling Alan McDonald's visit to our missionaries in Bogata.

18 May   HOW FAR CAN YOU GO?   St Paul went all the way across the Mediterranean to spread the gospel. How about you?

25 May   PLAYING THE FIELD Missionary Greg Toole shares more salacious tales from his heathen days (Tuesdays and Thursdays).

I also got a surprisingly good turnout when Sibling Doris Gray insisted on coming to bear witness to God's goodness to her during her recent hip operation. If you've got the accent, it's not hard to make 'Hip Op Night' sound rather more happening than it actually is.

Bible problems

I like to think that I'm fairly unshockable, but I have to say that the Bible knowledge of today's young people is scandalous. In my day, by the time we finished crèche we could recite the Lord's Prayer backwards – not that we ever did, because that would be satanic.

So I put my youth group and Sunday school on an intensive Bible-in-a-year Scripture reading programme, with an incentive scheme of tuck shop credits/public scourging. Unfortunately I had to stop it when parents complained about all the sex and violence I was making their children read.

This is why I produced the *Under 18s Bible* for my group, leaving out all the patriarchs getting legless, judicial tentpegging etc., and keeping all the bits about lambs and young people (not getting slaughtered). If you'd like some for your young people, I've still got plenty of them left. It's a lovely little book with large print, lots of pictures, and it still fits easily into the back pocket of their 501s.

* * *

The Rev. Testifies

Last March I took the whole Sunday school (the Crusaders, the Covenanters and the Inquisition) camping, and I ended up very depressed because nothing went wrong at all. No one got food poisoning, the PA system didn't blow up and no one nicked our mini-bus. Obviously it just wasn't good enough to be satanically attacked. Where had I gone wrong?

Then the Spirit spake unto me saying, 'Don't worry, Rev. Gerald. Your sinful depression is inspired by the evil one, so you are being satanically attacked after all. Well done.' So that was nice.

Ask the Rev.

Should I kiss my boyfriend on the first date? It's not like I'm ever likely to have one, but I'd like to know, just in case. And there doesn't seem to be anything in the Bible about it. There's some kissing in Song of Songs, but also lots of other things you wouldn't do on a first date. It also says Judas kissed Jesus, and some woman kissed his feet, but that isn't quite the same, is it?

SARAH BROOKS

The Rev. says:
This is disgusting! Honestly, what's a girl with a nice-sounding name like yours doing thinking about this kind of thing at your age? You should be thinking about sunsets and kittens, and nice Christian things like that. I never kissed a female of the opposite gender until I was ... well, ever, actually. So take a leaf out of my Bible.

There's this really nice girl in my youth group called Sandra, and I think the Lord wants us to go out together. But she says the Lord hasn't told her about it, and if he did she'd go and lie on the motorway.

I asked God for a definite answer, and I opened the Bible. It said, 'They cut off Saul's head, stripped off his armour, and sent messengers back with the good news.' I think that's a yes, because it would be good news for me, but Sandra says it's a no, for the same reason. What do you think?

                                                    JASON SINGER

The Rev. says:

What do you mean 'go out together'? Go where? Why don't you just go with your friends? What we do in our church if we can't agree about something, is split up into two different churches and never talk to each other again. That sorts out most problems. This isn't another question about kissing, is it?

My parents say that I definitely cannot get my eyebrow pierced, and that if I do then they will disown me. I am nearly 18 and I just want to express myself. It doesn't have anything about it in the Bible, so what do you say?

                                                    THOMAS WIENER

The Rev. says:

You must always do everything your parents tell you to do, because they are wise and good people. Unless they tell you something different from what I say, in which case they are evil and ignorant. Anyway, God has given you enough holes in your body without you making any more. Why don't you express yourself in words like normal people?

I just got the new Exploding Monks CD *Goin' Down the Chemist's* and it's really brilliant. But when I played it backwards it said 'oot slisperts emos em evig, ybab haey ho'. Do you think that's the Devil telling me to smoke drugs?

ELAINE BENDY

The Rev. says:
You mean you haven't been already? Does that mean you're naturally this weird? Well, if you listen to records by Catholics, you deserve all you get. How on earth do you get a CD to play backwards anyway?

How to save souls

'Evangelism' is a word from Greek roots: *ev*, meaning good; *angel*, meaning 'news'; and 'ism', meaning ministry. And that's what evangelism is: trying to persuade people that Christianity is good news, rather than depressing, made up and hypocritical. Why such a simple task should be so uncannily like banging your head against a brick wall, I just don't understand. Spiritual warfare, I suppose. Anyhow, there are many ways to do it, so let me guide you through them.

Street preaching

This method of sowing the holy seed has one huge advantage: you don't have to persuade anyone to come to a meeting or even read something. They can't escape it. They come down town to pop into Argos and the Nationwide, and they go home having had the Word of Truth opened up to them inescapably by a terrified church worker.

Warm up

Start off by singing some popular hymns to gather a crowd or at least take the edge off your nerves. Steer clear of anything too lengthy, negative or theologically abstruse. 'Amazing Grace' works well; my own judgmentological classic 'The 144 Storeys of Hell' has proved to be better suited to other work. And anything about crushing God's enemies should definitely be avoided, unless things go really badly.

The assault

Once the ice is broken, the anointed evangelist takes the megaphone. Use your own words, of course (or His own words, I should say!), but any anointed soul-saving sermon should cover all these points:

Hell

All bad people go to hell. All people are bad. So you're going to hell.

However good you are, you're still bad.

Hell is worse than the worst thing that you can possibly imagine. You might think the Shopping Channel is bad, but that's paradise compared to hell.

God

God loves us all more than you can possibly imagine. But still everyone whom he creates cannot fail to be condemned to hell. This is not God's fault, it's just life. (Explain the reasons for this in your own words.)

Heaven

Heaven is better than the best thing you can possibly imagine. Picture countless rows of pews stretching from one end of infinity to the other, with myriad blessed souls mumbling 'Lord I Lift Your Name on High' for the 11 trillionth time, some banging their heads on the pew in front in their enthusiasm, and reflecting that there are no fewer days to sing God's praise than when they'd first begun – and even that doesn't match it.

Salvation

You can't get to heaven by being good, so you can cut out that nonsense for a start. Salvation is an absolutely free gift from God. All you have to do to receive it is to believe the correct version of Christianity, join a theologically sound church, get baptized, and commit yourself to a lifetime of church attendance, prayer, Bible reading and tithing. And be predestined from before all eternity, of course.

Lay back-up

Few people in your church will have the gifting to say anything life-changing, soul-saving, or even remotely coherent when placed behind a microphone. Still, they have an important role to play, in their own way. While I street-preach, I have a couple of church members posted on street corners looking out for the police, while others ram Bibles down the throats of passers-by. Many have questioned the value of this Bible-ramming ministry, but Sibling Maureen knows of a man in her cousin's church who was converted by orally inserted Scripture, so I rest my case.

I also have several of the flock dressed as unbelievers to infiltrate the crowd of listeners, saying 'What do you think of this guy?', 'Hmm, that's a good point, isn't it?', and 'Well, he's convinced me. Shall we fall to our knees together in the Repentant Sinner's Prayer?' More often than not, to tell you the truth, these undercover workers are the crowd, and end up trying to force each other to their knees, but it's certainly better than evangelizing an empty precinct.

Results

Ideally, you will end up with a crowd of thousands weeping from conviction of sin and the joy of redemption. As often as not, though, you will have to look elsewhere for signs of success. When, instead of asking how they can be saved, most passers-by head into BHS, out the back, across the short-stay car park, and then back on to the street via Boots just to avoid walking past you, it can be easy to get discouraged. But I can truly say that wherever we go the police almost always move us on after an hour or two – and why would the Devil bother to attack us like that if we weren't doing some good?

Badge evangelism

This is the subtle approach. Many of your flock can be persuaded to wear a fish lapel badge in the hope that since in Greek the word 'fish' contains the initial letters of 'Jesus Christ Son of God Saviour', anyone who sets eyes on it will realize the truth of the gospel, despite the fact that they've never told anyone in their workplace that they go to church.

I tried wearing one myself for a while, and it did at least prove a conversation-starter. Conversations like:

'Interesting badge. Do you like fish?'

'No, but I like Jesus.'

'Bye then.'

Then I tried an even subtler approach:

'Interesting badge. Do you like fish?'

'Yes, and I sometimes go fishing on my day off.'

'Where do you...?'

'And you know, it's funny how much this simple sport, practised by many poor deceived worldlings, reflects the saving grace of the Almighty. The line is like his word, which he casts upon the waters of this world. The bait is the friendly approach of anointed evangelists like myself, the hook is his irresistible offer of grace to the undeserving (e.g. you), and the fish that land writhing and gasping on the bank are joyous souls safe at last on the dry ground of their local High Pentecostal-Reformed Church, evidently in an advanced state of charismatic blessing. So it's ironic that all I've ever caught are carrier bags.'

'Bye then.'

In the end I decided that a subtle badge of undercover Christianity is somewhat redundant on a cassock.

Mass evangelism

The idea of this more high-powered approach is that church members invite as many people as possible to come to Mass, where they will hopefully be so overwhelmed by the beauty of the liturgy, so enraptured by the tangible sense of earth touching heaven, and so high on the incense, that they will keep coming back. It has never been known to fail, or at least only in practice.

Crusade evangelism

This is the once fashionable technique of gathering hundreds of non-Christians together in one place and killing them and claiming their land and property for Jesus, as pioneered by such medieval figures as Count Guillaume de Grayham. The practice has fallen into disrepute, and a good thing too. Killing people is not evangelism! I could understand it if people were preached to first, and then dispatched to heaven before they had a chance to backslide, but this is jumping the gun.

Door to door

This is where you meet the enemy face to face, one to one – which is why you should always go out in pairs to halve the odds. Let's face it, we're not welcome, so we need some way of getting them into conversation before they slam the door. 'Taking a survey' is one ploy:

'Hello, we're doing a short survey of religious opinions. Would you mind taking part?'

'OK.'

'Right, question one: did you know that God loves you so much he sent Jesus to save you from your sins?'

'No.'

'Now that you do, what are you going to do about it?

(a) accept him into your heart;
(b) start going to Lewisham High Pentecostal-Reformed Church to find out more; or
(c) forget about it and go to hell?'

'Which do you suggest?'

Other good openers are:

'You don't know me, but I'm your son.'

'Excuse me, I'm lost. Can you give me directions?'

'Excuse me, you're lost. Can I give you directions?'

'Hello, madam, I'm Inspector Frosty and this is my assistant for the week WPC Ballotine. Do you mind if we come in or do you want to do this on the doorstep?'

'Hi, we're your new neighbours. Could we borrow some coffee?'

Once you get in, it's very easy to persuade them to turn from their life of misery, depravity and emptiness to the Christian life of joy, power and everlastingness, or at least it should be.

Mail shot

A circular letter is a good low-risk strategy for evangelism, allowing you to invite, challenge and testify without the trauma of meeting the not-yet-Christians on the receiving end. Here's an example for you from St U's, though it is of course copyright:

Dear Beloved Individual!

Congratulations! You may already be predestined to everlasting salvation!

You have been supernaturally selected from literally billions of living humans for an invitation to hear the word of truth!

Believe it or not, you have got through to the final round! All you have to do to qualify is to complete this 12-page booklet on your personal details, bring it to St Ursula's at 10.30 on Sunday morning, and listen to a short presentation from an official (almost) minister!

Imputed righteousness could be yours! Be the envy of your friends, family and other reprobates!

Don't delay! If you respond before 1 March, you will receive a free gift of the Spirit!

The Aleph course

Aleph is the brain and spirit child of Sibling Archie Thornton. This new way forward in evangelism was marvellously vouchsafed unto him by the Lord when he was rummaging about in the cupboard looking for the church water canon, and he found a file called 'Getting Fresh with God: The new Christians' course'. He started it up again, remarketing it as evangelism, and it has taken the High Pentecostal-Reformed world by storm.

Aleph is different from all other kinds of evangelism: we give people food. Admittedly missionaries in the Third World have often fed the starving, but at Aleph we feed the peckish. This is how we get them to sit through a sermon.

The pattern of pasta–sermon–discussion is so simple that churches across the country can all do it in whatever way suits them. Some play a video of me preaching the sermon, while the more adventurous read it out for themselves. And I give them complete freedom in their choice of pasta dishes (as long as they don't contain unbiblical food such as bacon, prawns and bats, of course!)

Each course starts with a launch party, and an introductory talk called 'Methodism: Boring, Untrue and Irrelevant'. The first week or two cover all the nagging problems of God, Jesus, creation, sin, suffering, other religions, etc. That leaves us free to go on to the

crucial nitty-gritty questions like 'How should I tithe?',
'What about fasting?' and 'Who is Rev. Gerald?'

The heart of Aleph is a weekend away where candidates
experience the full reality of High Pentecostal-Reformed
worship for themselves: the incense weekend. After
discussing 'What is Ol' Romanian?' and 'How do I use a
thurible?' we light up and have a sing, and one by one
people start panting, moaning, gasping and going down.
They come round with whole new sense of the presence
of God, and a bit of a headache.

The first time we ran the course at St U's, three people
actually became Christians, making it the most
successful evangelism I've ever been involved in. It hasn't
happened again, largely because all the non-Christians
that anyone knows came to the first one. To keep it
running I send all new church members through it, and
all old church members too. It fact it's been several years
since any non-believers attended, but at least it's still
going. And to be honest I prefer it like this. Believers ask
much better questions.

Ask the Rev.

> *I feel called to* save the Devil's soul. Do you know
> where I can find him?
>
> PATTY VALENTINE

The Rev. says:
Well, I expect he spends most of his time in brothels,
pubs and Lewisham Methodist Church, but that doesn't
mean you should. I believe the most reliable way of
getting hold of him is to draw a big circle and recite the
Bible backwards, but if I were you I'd make myself
scarce and leave a tract.

How to give your testimony

There is a more to a testimony than just telling your life story. For a start, if you only have three minutes, you have to leave an awful lot out. The purpose of a testimony is to persuade people that Christianity is a good thing, so include things that put God in a good light. Start with some examples of how evil and unhappy your life was before your conversion. Ideally this should include some crime, drug abuse, prostitution, suicide attempts (failed) or witchcraft. If you can't stretch that far, just make the most of what you've got.

Then you tell them how you became a Christian, which should be as sudden, dramatic and miraculous as you can make it. Finish off with a sentence or two about how blessed, whole and triumphant your life has been since then. I know you'll want to go on about the joys of the life of grace for ever, but for some incomprehensible reason that doesn't seem to make such a good story as knifings and devil worship. On the other hand, don't make the same mistake as the so-called evangelist Nina Goth who spoke at the Let Lewisham See Gerald mission, and got so carried away telling them about her days as a rock groupie she forgot to mention her conversion. Admittedly she shifted a lot of copies of her book *From Westlife to Eternal Life*, but that's hardly the point, is it?

Above all, don't complicate or confuse things by talking about being a good person before you were saved, or mentioning any doubts or failings you may have had since. Salvation is about turning from darkness to light. 'I was dead but now I am alive' is a good testimony; 'I was a bit poorly, but now I'm feeling a little better' is not.

Here is my own testimony for you to model yours on. (Don't copy it word for word. A testimony must be your own story, and mine is copyright.)

> The Lord has led me to share with you twisted and miserable heathens the story of how I came from being like you into this wonderful new life of grace and humble spiritual megastardom. Ideally you will be converted by this.

> I was born into a life of godless depravity. Of course, my parents went to chapel the usual three times on the Sabbath, and to five or so midweek meetings, but there was no real commitment there. My father was so blinded by unbelief he once told me that Scriptures like Psalm 78.65, 'Then the Lord woke from his sleep like a man waking from a drunken stupor', were not to be taken literally. And I once caught my mother reading

obviously unspiritual material on the Sabbath day, on the back of a cornflake packet.

Lo, things went from bad to worse, and soon I found myself eating black pudding, grasshoppers and liquorice – all clearly forbidden in the book of Leviticus, if you read between the lines. I began to doubt the infallibility of ancient Hebrew cosmology. I read the rude bits of the Bible in my quiet time. I watched television programmes, even some containing language and relations.

I could feel myself on the giddy path to the place of eternal fire and worms, where the fire burns for ever, but never burns up the worms, just kind of makes them hot, but without really punishing them, because they are the punishment, though to be honest it was the fire I was more worried about, really, than the worms. I never quite saw the point in the worms.

Then one day as I was walking down Lewisham High Street, absent-mindedly eating a sherbet fountain as I made rather unrealistic plans for debauchery, I heard a voice. And behold, there was a remarkably small one-eyed man standing on the school railings, yelling, 'Repent! Repent! The end of the world is so nigh, you wouldn't believe it. Repent! Or it's the worms for you.'

His challenging words truly touched my soul. Moments later this holy saint was killed in a tragic impaling accident, but knowing that the Lord had spared him long enough to bring truth into my darkness, I threw away my liquorice stick and, stopping only to perform a minor feeding miracle, I walked on into everlasting blessing.

I cannot say that since then life has been a bed of roses, because when you think about it a rose bed is a stupidly uncomfortable place, and Christianity is just brilliant.

How to have a beach mission

There are two kinds of mission: soul and body. One delivers people from the everlasting tortures of hell to everlasting joy, wholeness and hymn singing; the other makes improvements to the few paltry years of their life here below, while they cheerfully head to perdition. What's more, it's a well-known fact that the poor and miserable respond more positively to the gospel, so the more you give them food and clothes the less likely they are to turn to God. From this, it is not hard to see which kind of mission is more Christian.

I must admit that at St U's Sibling Ken Stamp used to have a mission to beggars, taking his van down town every Monday night and handing out cans of Special Brew and cigarettes. He claimed to have a real heart for the homeless, but I put a stop to it because I could tell he just had a real heart for getting out of the Monday night prayer meeting.

It is simply counter-productive, being nice to people. The only thing worse is being nice to the planet. True Christians long for the day when the earth will be destroyed with fire. Saving the ozone layer is only for those who prefer earth to heaven.

For several years I have devoted two weeks a year to my one-man (and his God) Ibiza beach mission. I would be more than happy to set the details of the work before you as a template for new outreaches to centres of sun, sin and sandcastles from Bournemouth to Bermuda.

Youth work

Mornings are devoted to youngsters. Most people don't realize how responsive teenagers are to the wondrous gospel message. So after the day's activity, I read them a related Bible story: sandcastle competition/the Tower of Babel; free swim/parting the Red Sea; another sandcastle competition/the wise man who built his house upon the rock.

And the things they come out with! During that last session, a girl once asked me 'Why do you illustrate a story about the futility of building houses on sand by making us do the same thing?' Kids, eh? They're enthusiastic, but they don't know where to draw the line. Sometimes you have to hit them full on with the truth of the redemption story; sometimes you just have to hit them.

Prayer

Knowing the spiritual warfare that lies ahead in the afternoon, I then spend a couple of hours each day in a quiet corner of the beach, prostrated in anguished intercession for the lost holidaying souls of Ibiza. Anointed from head to foot in St Ambrose Solaire sinblock factor 36, you might mistake me for just another pagan sunbather, if it weren't for the unmistakable aura of holiness, my Jesus Saves swimming trunks and, of course, the dog collar.

Finally, wrapping my missal and *Ten Famous Missionary Scandals* paperback in my towel, I put the cassock back on and return to work.

Naturist outreach

Afternoons take me to the very heart of the Enemy's stronghold: the nudist beach. Edging along the wall at the top with my back to the kitless heathen, I hurl fistfuls of tracts over my shoulder at them: *Repent and Repant*, *Groinal Nakedness, the Sin of Noah*, and *You'll Never Be Raptured with Your Bits Out*. I sling the odd hymnbook as well. I've got plenty we don't use at St U's any more, so you might as well put them to a good cause. You never know what will come of it if God is in it. Of course, this ministry faces strong opposition – though not as much as when I used to do it walking through the middle of the beach blindfolded.

I have been given a real heart for nudists. A lot of people think they're a lost cause, but I've seen some outstanding members among them. Really, they're trying to get back to before the fall, and you've got to respect that. Not that I would ever consider going among them as one of their own; that would be taking incarnational missiology too far. This flesh is not for flashing.

Clubbing

Even when the the sun sets on this pagan paradise, I rest not, continuing my labours in unquenchable faith that one day someone will listen to me. And so to the nightclub.

It has been remarked upon, though I say it myself, that my dancing is testimony to the fact that I have not squandered much of my time in this godless activity. You have to try to fit in, though. I spent several evenings at Sibling Maureen Crank's liturgical dance workshop earlier this year, and I think it paid off.

So, concealing my priestly vestments under a cagoule, I mingle among the multitude, raising my hands aloft in what I trust is time to the music, handing out copies of *But I Never Thought I'd Be Damned for Wine Gums!*, and *The Collected Proverbs of Rev. Gerald Ambulance*, remembering from a couple of unfortunate experiences not to take any sweets from anybody.

Finally I return to my little room to receive the Lord's blessing of sleep to empower me for another day's spiritual warfare. Yes, I rejoice in the knowledge that the word of the Lord does not return unto Him void, but accomplishes that which He pleases, and doth prosper in the thing whereto He sent it, though it usually seems to wait till I'm gone before it does.

Ask the Rev.

The game's up, Rev. I know all about your so-called 'beach mission'. The truth has been uncovered – and more than just the truth, eh?

Here's the deal. None of us wants to read any more salacious stories about vicars in the Sunday papers, so just transfer 50 per cent of your treasure in heaven over to me (New Jerusalem, PO Box 3781318534531), and I'm sure the whole thing will blow over.

SIBLING X

The Rev. says:
Congratulations, Sibling X, on the most incomprehensible utterance since Maurice Zabbo attempted to post in tongues by typing with his forehead while under the influence of Ol' Romanian.

How to have a revival

Here is the Rev.'s ten-step recipe:

1 Tarry until the Hour of Prophetic Readiness – when churches across the land proclaim that revival is finally coming upon us. (Shouldn't be long now.)
2 Have a few more prophecies just to make sure.
3 Set a date for your revival. (Sunday evening is a particularly anointed time.)
4 Advertise it in the Christian press, to declare unto God your truly mountainous faith, and to get a better turnout.
5 On the big night, lift all hearts up to the heavenlies, with the latest in funky Christian music. (If this proves too much for your organist, hire extra musicians from the RGA Ministries Revival Agency.)

6 Keep it up till your congregation are on the floor hyper-ventilating and making farmyard animal noises. You might want to include 'Old MacDonald' in your worship songs to get people warmed up. However, bear in mind that the Spirit may have gone off this particular way of winning the hearts of men (and women these days!), so be open to whatever may come, whether it be the blessing of gold teeth, navel-piercing or breast implants, or a new wave of pogo-ing, bungee jumping or breakdancing.

7 Ideally your meeting will now be so full of the presence of the Almighty Spirit of Celestial Outpouring that it will flood out into the surrounding region and convert everybody as soon as you open the door. In practice, it might take a bit more time. So you all tell everyone you meet about your life-changing night of gasping, barking and supernatural dentistry. They all say, 'Although I previously thought Christianity was a bit sad and weirdo, I now realize this is what I've been waiting for all my life!'

8 Next Sunday, everyone in the neighbourhood will come longing to drink deep of the wells of salvation and ready for a good cluck/bounce/bust enhancement, etc.

9 Keep going until everyone has spread it around everywhere, ushering in a new age of universal salvation, world peace and really cool worship songs.

10 Don't forget to take the offering!

Ask the Rev.

One of the bits on my gold-plated charm bracelet has turned kind of white. Could this the first example of

God turning gold into teeth?

ALICE CORDUROY

The Rev. says:
What are you doing with a charm bracelet? That's the work
of Beelzebub! True Christians have nothing to do with
charm at all. Anyone who believes in superstition will be
cursed by God.

How to hatch, match and dispatch

It is an unwelcome irony (though of course all irony is unwelcome) that most people are as determined to have the clergy involved in the three most important events of their life as they are not to have them involved in any other part of it. Here is how to go about them.

Christening

There has been much debate in the High Pentecostal-Reformed Church of late as to whether we should baptize only the children of true, tithing believers, or anyone who wants it. Happily I can settle this dispute. It is a good rule of thumb that when two sides disagree the truth tends to lie somewhere violently to the extreme of one of them, and both in a very real sense are wrong.

In this case the truth is that we should baptize everyone, and not just those who want it. Hit-and-run baptism has long been an integral part of my beach mission. And with my Super-Spirt-U-All Holy Water Pistol under my alb, even a stroll down the high street presents manifold opportunities to be an agent of unsought regeneration.

Some weaker siblings have questioned whether it is biblical to use guerrilla tactics in the administration of the sacraments. But doth not the psalmist say 'Bless the Lord'? And what could bring greater blessing unto Him before Whom we are all but as picture interference on the superfluous fifth channel of this world, than washing the unwary into the Kingdom?

I also like to re-christen any who come into the church with unbiblical 'Christian' names. This has provoked an ungodly rumpus from the usual troublemakers, on the grounds of 'hypocrisy'. May I point out once and for all the blindingly obvious fact that 'Gerald' is my middle name, and my Christian name features in hundreds of Bible verses from Rev. 1.1 to Rev. 22.21.

Marriage

Marriage and burial are without a doubt the saddest and happiest parts of this job: launching brothers and sisters into their new life of bliss, love and spiritual blessings in the case of burial, and condemning them to decades of antagonism and stress with the distractions of pointless fleshly pleasures ever preying on them in the case of marriage.

The simple fact is that not everyone is up to the glorious

life of celibacy to which I have been so joyously called. If only more were content to be as I am, wed to the Almighty (the only kind of same-sex marriage sanctioned by the Scriptures)! But sad though it is to see once mighty warriors apostatize from their ministry of singleness, marriage is not all bad. It is necessary for the Church to be reproducing in order to keep the Sunday school going, and to bring a new generation up in the faith to make up for our inability to convert adults.

There was even a time when I sought the Lord about the idea of walking in such paths myself, taking unto myself a godly woman, or even an Old Testament-style patriarchal harem, in order to populate the world with a holy army of the sons of Gerald. But all the signs are that the Lord considers my own uninterrupted work more important to the Kingdom than anything procreation can achieve. (If you hear any different from the Lord, then contact me via www.ship-of-fools.com. No nutters, please.)

In the meantime, having been saved from the perils and defilement of the married state or anything remotely like it, I am ideally placed to offer guidance and instruction to those who succumb, steering Christian couples through the pitfalls of courtship into the pit of matrimony.

These are the obligatory guidelines I give to young men involved in pre-married coupling in St Ursula's:

1   No touching. A bird in the hand is worth 75 years in Purgatory. I don't want to get legalistic about this, and holding hands is not in itself quite a sin, but I am reliably informed that all physical contact between the sexes is an explosive slippery slope drawing you down towards a dark hidden pit of profane euphoria. And you don't want that now, do you?

2   Wear a minimum 25 items of clothing whenever you are together. If you feel especially weak, the WWJD? boxer shorts are a must, with sewn up fly and picturing the Virgin Mary looking sad. For young ladies, RGA Ministries also provide WWMD? undergarments and an invaluable body map tattoo, dividing their flesh into zones of sinfulness, with slogans like 'You are now entering the damnation zone.'

3   No kissing, except figuratively. If your intended says she wants you to kiss her, you should assume she knows – being immersed in the language of Scripture – that 'Let him kiss me with the kisses of his mouth' expresses the willingness of the Christian soul to receive strictly spiritual blessings from above (the only kind worth having and the only direction worth having them from), and therefore simply desires you to impart some much needed prayerful ministry unto her soul. Tell her you are ready to serve, and let the laying on of hands commence. Do not exercise the gift of tongues.

4   Never be together in the same room without other people there (or at all preferably).

5   No rumpy-pumpy. Virginity is the most priceless jewel a woman can wear, the most valuable asset she can sign over to her husband upon marriage, the cherry on the icing of the cake of femininity. The quality of not having experienced gynaecological satisfaction is worth infinitely more than devoting your life to medical care, education or the abolition of world poverty.

And this is my expert advice for brothers who marry:

1   Lay down your biblical authority as a man, and show

her who's boss from the very beginning: whenever she tells you to do something, do the opposite. If there isn't an opposite, just use your imagination. Then tell her you did what she said. If she ever finds out that you didn't, and challenges you, just pretend you don't speak English. This has never been known to fail.

2   If she complains, just say, 'Who was created first?'

3   Every time you come home from work, hit your wife with an extraordinarily large piece of polystyrene. It's the only language they understand.

4   Start your married life off with a full and frank discussion about you-know-what, without, as far as possible, any direct reference to parts of the body or other things. Let your beloved get this unpleasant necessity behind her once and for all so she will never need to face the whole disagreeable subject again.

5   Marital encounters without the object of begetting are not on, if you know what I mean. You probably don't. What I'm saying is that prophylacticism is an abomination before the Lord. For doeth not 2 Samuel 20.8 say, 'And Joab's sword was fastened upon his loins in the sheath thereof; and as he went forth it fell out'? I think it's quite clear what that's getting at. Obviously it is the duty of every Christian couple to contribute to the worldwide population explosion that promises to destroy civilization and hasten the Day of the Lord.

6   Never forget those three wonderful words that, however many times you say them, will never fail to take your relationship back to where it belongs: 'Where's my dinner?'

Burial

This is a lot simpler. You don't need to give advice or instruction about the afterlife. (Well, of course you do, it's your whole reason for existing, but by this point the recipient is unlikely to benefit much from even the best advice.) All you need to do is lower the deceased into the ground and set up a stone announcing who they were and telling them to RIP (standing for 'rest in peace' or 'roast in Purgatory', depending). In theory there are the grieving relatives to cope with too, but in practice they rarely turn to the clergy for consolation, or not in my experience anyway.

How to be guided

St Botolph of Boston said that spiritual maturity is learning to use for ourselves our own minds under the enlightenment of the Holy Ghost. Which is utter garbage, because spiritual maturity is learning never to trust your own mind and signing all decision-making responsibilities over to Him before Whom we are all, even I, but as the irritating but inaccessible semi-hardened phlegm of time in the nasal passage of eternity. If God had meant us to think for ourselves, he would have given us brains that work properly. For doeth not the Scripture say, 'Listen not unto thine heart, for thou mayst strain thy neck'? If not, it's the kind of thing that it would have said, if it had been just a bit longer. So let me talk you through the three infallible ways of discerning the celestial steer.

Bibliomancy

Before you seek the Lord, it is essential to get yourself into a spiritually receptive frame of mind. Light a candle, burn some Ol' Romanian and put on some truly holy music – I almost always go for *Let Me Be a Living Mountain* by the Tim Splendid Worship Trio (£14.99 from RGA Ministries).

Then take up a Bible. It is God's word and perfect in every way, so whatever you need to know will be in there, as long as you know how to find it. Say this prayer with perfect faith:

Mighty God, 'tis up to Thee
Show me what Thou'd'st say to me.

Then open the Bible, and read the verse that your Spirit-guided eyes fall upon. It may not be immediately obvious how the verse answers your query, but meditate upon it with prayer and deep breathing, and something will come to mind. If it doesn't, you must have picked a dud verse, demonstrating the woeful inadequacy of your faith. Either that or your question was too horrifyingly unspiritual for the Lord to answer. Either way, neither he nor I are in any way to blame.

The saints

Not only are they now within God's earshot, what with being in heaven and everything, but the saints know just what it's like to live a real human life – especially a real human life up a 60-foot pole or in a cave in the Egyptian desert. (Apart from the ones that never literally existed, who just have to use their imagination.) What's more, they all have their specialist areas: St Anthony, patron saint of lost stuff, will help you find your video remote, St Christopher will get you through the Catford one-way system, and St Swithun will advise you when to plan your church picnic.

The Church has made thousands of these appointments over the centuries, of course, so some questionable ones are only to be expected. St Sebastian is patron saint of archers, for example, which is a bit insensitive considering how he died. (In recent centuries he has been in semi-retirement, of course, and nowadays spends most of his time as continuity adviser to *The Archers*.) And St Joseph is patron saint of fathers, which, when you consider the whole point of the Christmas story, is a clear case of not what you know but whom you know.

To claim the help of the beatific assembly, consult the Rev. Gerald Ambulance Invocation Table (£6.99 from RGA Ministries) to find out who has the expertise you need and how to address them. Prostrate yourself before an image of the saint in an attitude of devout but non-idolatrous veneration, and light a candle. Better still, light a candle in the shape of the saint whose help you seek. Avoid martyrs who were burnt at the stake, though, as this often irritates rather than invoking them.

WWGD?

The most reliable way of all to find the true path is to get yourself a WWGD? digital watch. Handsomely inscribed in large pink letters, the watch constantly reminds you of the question that guides your every step as a truly born-of-the-blood, biblically baptized, Bible-believing believer: What would Gerald do?

More to the point, it answers the question for you. Whatever your problem, dilemma or doubt, just press the button, and the infallibly spooky voice of Rev. Gerald in full ministry utters forth: 'Don't wrestle, just nestle.' 'Give it up. It's disgusting.' 'Go to church.' 'Don't thrust, just trust.' 'Sell your possessions and give the money to the poor.' Never again will you be left in the dark about the Lord's glorious will for your miserable little existence, unless the batteries go.

I should also mention that if your behaviour is particularly unsound, the watch may speak forth unto you, without you even pressing the button. RGA Ministries cannot be held responsible for any embarrassment or personal troubles caused. You deserve whatever you get.

The WWGD? Deluxe also has a sinshocker™ feature. In the unlikely event of the wearer ignoring the Geraldic advice, it will aid your conscience by administering a small electric shock. The size of the shock varies in relation to the seriousness of the sin. In the case of injury or death, again, you deserve it.

Ask the Rev.

I think God's calling me to be unemployed. I keep asking him what I should do when I leave college, and he keeps saying nothing.

ADAM CHIMNEY

The Rev. says:
So what's your question?

How to write worship songs

Many of you, I know, consider me one of the most anointed songwriters in history, but I must deny that. Yes, my songs have often changed your lives, your hearts, your bank balance and your denominational allegiance. But I am not the true writer, for the Holy Spirit wrote them through me. Let the glory not go unto me, who am but a big fish to spew forth the Jonah of God's gifts.

However, I have learnt a lot in the process about what makes my songs the best, so if that's your ministry, read and feed.

Switch off

You must learn to become an empty vessel, a mere tube for the toothpaste of the Lord. Get into a worshipful frame of mind – or worshipful frame of spirit, rather, and vacate your mind completely. Then whatever comes into your head first will inevitably be from God. Light a candle, burn some incense (the stronger the better – you can't beat Ol' Romanian celestial strength), and float downstream. Remember, the Spirit loves a vacuum. A vacant head and vacuous lyrics give him room to move.

This one I knew without a doubt was from the Lord, because I woke up with the words on my mind in the middle of a sermon (that someone else was preaching):

O God, you're really Lord.
Jesus, you're really Lord.
Spirit, you're really Lord.
I'm glad you don't get bored.

And Lord you really are just really Lord (x 12)

Don't worry if what comes out sounds a bit banal or meaningless to you. When you think about it, the whole human race must seem banal to God, so who are we to judge? And with a bit of providence the punters singing it will be too out of their heads and into the heavenlies to mind.

Words and stuff

If this doesn't work, you'll have to come up with something yourself. First pick your subject. There are two different subjects you can write songs about: who God is, and the fact that we're worshipping him.

To do the first, start off with 'O Lord you are...', or 'He is so...'. Then say something nice about God. There are plenty of words to choose from, 53 in fact. Just flick through *Songs of Siblinghood* and you'll soon learn them.

The second subject is just as easy. Start with 'I really want to...' or 'Lord, we just...', and stick in any one of the many synonyms God has given us for 'worship'. When you get the hang of these two, you can even combine them in one song. Here's a song that will give you plenty of ideas:

We raise, exalt and magnify,
Lift up, promote and bless your name,
We elevate and glorify:
I bet you're glad we came.

And now we give you adoration,
Worship, glory, thanks and prayer,
Majesty and deity:
Hello, are you still there?

Being original

Please don't. The world of contemporary worship lyrics has gone 30 years without a single original image, and we don't need you to start now. If you want to get flowery, the song book is full of tried and tested clichés which we know God likes because they're from the Bible. He wants us to sing about towers, shepherds, chains, sacrifices, kings, swords, idols and timbrels. What could be more unspiritual than singing to God about things that didn't happen in the ancient Middle East?

To make sure that nothing of you gets into the song, but only what is of the Lord, simply lift a verse out of the Bible.

Forget the context. Don't change a thing, even if it starts in the middle of a sentence. It will still be meaningful – it's Scripture.

This one is a good example:

But glory, honour and peace *(Men)*
But glory, honour and peace *(Women)*
For everyone that does good *(Under-30s)*
For everyone that does good *(Over-30s)*
But glory, honour and peace *(Left-handed people)*
But glory, honour and peace *(Right-handed people)*
For everyone that does good *(Calvinists)*
For everyone that does good *(Arminians)*
First for the Jew *(Circumcised and virgins)*
First for the Jew *(Uncircumcised and wives)*
Then for the Gentile *(Together)*

Mood

There are two to choose from: upbeat, positive and uplifting, or mellow, positive and uplifting. Using them you can cover the whole range of Christian feelings, from confidence to thankfulness, from joy to serenity, and from excitement to awe.

Admittedly, some less victorious Christians do sometimes experience less spiritual feelings – unhappiness, confusion, anger, doubt, etc. – but we shouldn't encourage such things by letting people admit to them in church. I assure you God wants nothing to do with that part of their lives, and neither do I. It's exactly the kind of thing I go to church to take my mind off.

Which of the following songs would raise your spirit in anointed worship? The outpouring of praise mostly by me (with some insignificant contributions from the pen of Sibling David Perry) or the godless twaddle by Bill Sweetie?

Oh Lord I'm 110 per cent on fire for you night and day,
I'm so hyped up I just want to fall down for no reason.
I want to praise till I'm dizzy from it,
I want to worship till I vomit,
And I know this hysteria will last for ever.

When I stand in your presence today,
I feel just about OK.

The one way to let negative stuff into your song, if you really know what you're doing, is to start off saying, 'Oh dear, look at all the problems out there in the non-Christian world', and end by saying 'Never mind though, Jesus has sorted everything out'.

All this means that, as a songwriter, there are certain psalms you should avoid. If you must use one of the miserable ones, skip to the end where things usually brighten up. Steer well clear of Psalm 88, though: yes, God-breathed Scripture and all that, but no one in 2000 years has based a hymn on it, and we don't want to start now.

Hymns

Many churches who use contemporary worship resources have also been rediscovering the riches of hymns from past ages. To stop this getting out of hand and overshadowing what the Lord is doing in our days through you, why not try your hand at your own *Hymns Ancient and Neolithic*? You need a plodding rhythm, bad rhymes and some 300-year-old vocabulary:

Wert Ephraim's bondage not beheld,
Thy ransom'd pascal blood,
Vouchsafe yon blessèd cherubim;
Henceforth redeem'd we stood.

Mumble mumble mumble mumble mumble hallelujah.

Marching songs

These are a wondrous way to finish a service, getting the
congregation tanked up on the Spirit, ready to march forth
in faith and have their Sunday lunch in triumph.

This is the kind of tone to aim at:

We are marching out, marching out, marching out upon
the land,
With a helmet on our head and a sword in our hand.
We'll stab their guts and break their heads,
And we'll be alive and they'll be dead.
Oh we are so gung-ho for the Lord.

We are stepping forth, stepping forth, stepping forth to
claim the ground.
We'll curse them when they're up and convert them when
they're down.
Our enemies fall in consternation,
We celebrate their eternal damnation.
Oh we are so gung-ho for the Lord.

We are bombing them, bombing them, bombing them
from above,
But please don't be alarmed for we're doing it in love.
First we'll chastise and rebuke them,
But if that doesn't work we'll have to nuke them.
Oh we are so gung-ho for the Lord.

Music

There's not much to say about the music. It's only the words that matter, and I'm sure whatever tune comes into your head will be from the Lord, even if it does bear an uncanny resemblance to the last thing you heard on the radio.

Two points:

1 Avoid minor keys, because they can sound a little negative. However, if you know what you're doing, there are two ways you can use them:

(a) Have the verse in a minor key, and then when the chorus changes to the major it will sound even more happy. See if you can spot where the key change comes in this one:

I walked the path of death and woe,
Of misery and sin.
Despite the fun and happiness,
Life was meaningless within.

But Jesus turned my trudging into skipping,
He has turned my dryness into sipping,
Jesus turned my drowning into shipping,
He turned my unchastity to zipping.
He has turned my life about,
Inside down and upside out,
And everything is lovely now for me.

I walked the downward path to hell,
Heading to damnation,
Making rather optimistic
Plans for fornication.

(b) Give the song an authentic ancient Hebrew feel by having a minor key, an offbeat rhythm, references

to tambourines, tents and timbrels, a verse of la la
las, dee dee dees or dum dum dums, and a final
rousing cry of 'Oyvez!'

2 Borrow music from secular songs. You can change a bit
here and there and call it a completely different song.
Alternatively you can just lift the whole tune and set new
words to it. There are copyright issues here, but the way
I look at it (a) how is the composer of 'Twist and Shout'
going to find out what you sing in your church? (b) how
can anything be unethical when you do it for the glory
of God? and (c) it's all the Devil's music anyway, and the
Prince of Darkness is fair game.

This one is a firm favourite at St U's. Apparently the
music is from the theme song of a particularly worldly
American comedy series:

We always told you life was gonna be this way;
Your life's a futile mess now since you went astray.
Why don't you turn back to the Holy One?
He'll cleanse you, ransom you, and fill you with his Son.

He'll be there for you when you're tempted to fall.
He'll be there for you when the Evil One calls.
He'll be there for you like he's there for me too.

God invented hell for people who do what you do.
He burned the Rich Man, do you think that he'll spare you?
The Bible warned you there'd be days like these.
You've got no hope unless you get on to your knees.

He'll be there for you when you witness at work.
He'll be there for you when you act like a jerk.
He'll be there for you like he's there for me too.

He'll be there for you when you feel like a drink.
He'll be there for you when you're tempted to think.
He'll be there for you like he's there for me too.

(Words by Rev. Gerald Ambulance and
Sibling David Perry)

Ask the Rev.

The Lord has given me a worship song, but everyone in
my church says it's a total pile of pants. How can I make
them sing it?

BARRY COLLINS

The Rev. says:
One of my congregation, Sibling Bill Sweetie, had a similar
problem. Whenever we had open worship, he started
bellowing it out, often in the middle of other songs,
constantly crying, 'Come on everybody!' If you too want to
get locked in the underfloor baptistery until the next
baptism, that's what I'd suggest.

Smile!

Jesus loves you!

How to be relevant

It is vitally important, they tell me, to be relevant to people's lives, to build bridges into the community and to talk to folk in their own language. I've never seen it myself. After all, the Spirit talks to us in tongues, and we don't mind.

In my experience, what they mean when they bang on about sermons being relevant to their lives is that they want less about the Bible and more jokes. To be fair, though, I take the point about building bridges into the community, as some of the older members of St U's do find it difficult crossing the moat on a Sunday morning.

Anyway, after much nagging from these progressive types about meeting people's needs, I agreed to a survey of local people asking them why they don't come to our church. The general answer seemed to be 'Because it's rubbish'. They had countless very negative criticisms that showed they were utterly hardened to the work that the Lord is doing in our days, so I called an extraordinary church meeting to burn effigies of everyone who partook in the survey.

And that, I assumed, was the end of the matter. But when I returned from my Ibiza beach mission a couple of months later, I found they'd gone and listened to these carpers and critics, and Sibling Bill Sweetie had led them in some kind of relevant revolution. They had given my beloved St Ursula's a massive multi-hundred-pound new look, and attempted to turn it into a kickin', in yer face, happ'nin' joint. (But not with any actual face-kicking, admittedly, or joints.)

So here, for those of you who also feel the need to sell out to the spirit of the age, is how they gave the church a makeover.

Name

Apparently St Ursula's High Pentecostal-Reformed Church is a very sad and boring name, so they chose one that was full of religious symbolism but subtle enough that no one would ever notice: 'Joe's Kebab Bar'. Joe is (in this case) short for Joshua, whose name means 'saviour', and Jesus is the saviour of the world. Kebabs are made of lamb, and Jesus is the lamb of God. And *bar* is Hebrew for 'son', and Jesus is the Son of God.

'We're proclaiming the name of Jesus,' explained Bill, 'for those who have ears to hear, but in a seeker-friendly way that doesn't put people off.'

Buildings

They pulled down the notice board out front with the times of services, the names and theological positions of the deacons and a list of the ten most dangerous heresies taught by local churches. In its place was a pink neon sign saying, 'Hi There!' Believe it or not it also said, 'Learn to tango at the Rivoli Ballroom', because the sign cost rather more than expected, and they needed a sponsor.

Inside, they had got rid of all the rows of pews looking up at the pulpit. It seems the old set-up had a 'him up there and us down here' feel to it. Well, dur! 'Plus they give you butt ache,' as Sibling Lou Jolly so righteously put it. Instead there were beanbags dotted about the room, with coffee tables bearing glossy books full of photos of Israel. 'We've got more books on order', explained Bill, 'about other nice-looking places created by God, and cute animals of the kind that might have been on the ark.'

I can't say I was particularly sorry to see the banners had come down, with all those mindnumbingly literal pictures of the fruits of the Spirit. Unfortunately they had replaced them with even more banners, based on classic bumper stickers, like 'If you can read this, thank the Lord for your eyes!', 'Baby Jesus on board' and 'My other church is a Strict Amalgated Peruvian Congregationalist'.

In place of the Ten Commandments, there was a flipchart with the week's top ten. There was a drinking fountain where the font used to be. And to top it all the altar was gone, along with the few simple instruments of humble New Testament worship that graced it: the chalice, the candlesticks, the purificator, the cruets, the paten, the lavabo, the pyx, the reredos, the aspergillium, the predella, the faldstool, the crotalus, the credence, the monstrance, the thecla, the scotula, the triptych, and that big mushroom that I've never worked out what to do with. And in their place was some fearful piece of modern 'art' that may conceivably have been a picture of our Lord, but might just as easily have been a still life of squashed frog and spanners. Call that progress? Because I don't.

Services

Fortunately they hadn't got round to having any yet, but the idea was 'to radically revise the whole approach to sermons'. By not having any. Apparently people today just can't relate to 30-minute speeches, so instead of sermons they were going to have TV. Where the pulpit used to be, there would be a big screen, to show films which touch on religious topics in a non-threatening way, such as *Prince of Egypt*, *The Exorcist*, and *The Life of Brian*, and episodes of the Simpsons where they go to church.

A 10p-sized wafer and a thimbleful of grape juice not being a cool and groovy snack, communion was to be re-imagined in the form of assorted dips on the coffee tables, and various tasty non-alcoholic alternatives such as Dr Pepper's and 7Up. And for the creed, they would sing 'I Believe I Can Fly' by R Kelly.

The Bible

'I've done a bit of editing,' Bill told me. 'I think we can all agree there's a lot of information there we can do without. So I've come up with an easy-going new version that tells all the good stories in an up-to-date way that makes sense to today's world.'

Let me give a you a reading from this abomination of desolation:

Adam and Eve lived in a garden with lots of talking animals. One day their friend Snake said,

'How come you never eat the apples from the tree in the middle of the garden?'

'Dunno,' said Eve. 'They look kinda funny.'

'That's coz they're extra special apples full of appley goodness. Don't worry, they're not GM.'

'No,' said Eve. 'I don't really fancy them.'

'Look, if you eat one of these, you'll be superhuman. You'll have the Knowledge. You'll know the difference between good and not quite so good. And you'll have lots of friends and look sexy.'

And so Eve bit the apple, and behold it was just another boring Granny Smith. 'That's the last time I believe adverts,' she said.

And she gave one to Adam. And he bit it and said, 'I quite like them actually.'

Then they moved to somewhere with better facilities and a longer lease. And they all lived happily ever after.

So that's how to be trendy and up to date. I'm sure it has its advantages, but when the disadvantages are desecrating the sanctuary of the Most High, emasculating the gospel, and going behind the back of the minister, the advantages don't count for much. Let us linger then, siblings, in the asylum of our holy refuge, where any influence between us and the world either way is kept to a minimum.

How to do spiritual gifts

As an anointed labourer in the vineyard of the Almighty, it is vital that you lead your flock into the fullness of spiritual gifts. So first you must develop as many gifts as you can yourself, as visibly as possible, to spur them on.

The gift of tongues

This is the Spirit's number one plan for your voicebox. Honesty and encouragement and suchlike are also good, but nothing adds to the worship of the church like a bit of unintelligibility. What a joy it is to minister to our beloved with tongues, and touch the parts that other ministries can't reach!

If you're having trouble getting started, here are a few handy expressions from my *Glossolalia Phrasebook* to get you going:

Tongues	English
Coriander vishnu à la kalashnikov mitsubishi!	God loves you, and wants you to really surrender your fear, and go forward into a time of deep blessing.
Kawasaki ashterah allah vespa salami!	God really wants you to surrender to his love, so don't fear to go forward into a deep time of blessing.
Coriander coriander coriander coriander coriander coriander coriander hare krishna bazooki!	God loves deep blessing, so don't be afraid to surrender to a time of really going forward.
Allelujah!	Vote Labour.

The gift of interpreting tongues

If you want the gift of interpretation, you can use the chart backwards.

At St Ursula's, after the weekly Latin Mass, Sibling Elaine Chutney always brings an interpretation. Apparently, it usually means that God is not afraid to surrender blessings unto us, so we should go deeply forward into a really lovely time, or something. Other times, though, it turns out to be a surprisingly detailed oracle against the sins of her sister Eileen, especially when she sits too near the thurifer.

The gift of prophecy

There are two kinds of prophetic utterance, both wondrous blessings in their own way, but one is a lot safer than the other:

Words from the Lord

This is a piece of cake. You say, 'I just really feel the Lord is saying…', and then you say something that you just really feel the Lord is saying. It's not hard to think of something:

> 'There's someone here who really just needs to know that He loves them and wants them to open up to Him.'

> 'It's time to take a stand against the Enemy, and claim release from everything that is not of God'.

Vague but plausible is the key here. The kind of thing that on the hundred to one chance that it's not true, no one could ever pin it on you.

There are two styles to choose from: (a) encouraging; and (b) rebuking, but also quite encouraging. The Lord certainly has a much more positive attitude to His people these days than in the Old Testament, and that's nice.

Foretelling the future

This is a lot trickier. Believe me, prophecies of Armageddon can really blow up in your face. My own much misunderstood series of books *1990s: Last Days on Planet Earth*, *1999: The Final Countdown* and *2001: Extension Granted!* are a case in point. Still, the Lord has taught me a valuable lesson through it, and I won't make the same mistake again – even if my *2020 and That's Final* were to prove wrong, it wouldn't be for 20 years, and that's two decades of much needed royalties for the work of the Kingdom.

You should probably steer away from the whole 'the end of the world is so nigh you wouldn't believe it' business. If you get it wrong you look like a right donkey, and if you get it right, who's going to be patting you on the back?

Revival is a much better bet. Here, vague and conditional is the key. 'Revival is coming to Milton Keynes on 13 March and 1,816 people will be converted' is asking for trouble. Go for 'It's just around the corner, if we but humble ourselves before Him.' This approach has stood faithful revival watchers in good stead for decades.

In the unlikely event that some unspiritual doubter questions you, e.g. demanding to know why over the last ten years of revival-prophecy church attendance has dropped by 25 per cent, just cry,

'You've got a spirit of rebellion! You haven't humbled yourself! Siblings, gather round. This is the unhumbled soul who lost our revival.' From there it's plain sailing.

The gift of knowledge

It's such a blessing to bring a word that really speaks into someone's situation, but again there are pitfalls. As ever, woolliness is the answer: 'You have a spirit of unitarianism', or 'You have an unclaimed gift of worm collecting', not 'You commit unspeakable atrocities with Danish pastries, and your video remote's down the back of the fridge.'

If you must be specific, probe:

'I see there is someone in your life who's going through a hard time, is that right?'

'Yes. Charlie.'

'That's right, Charlie. And you're quite close to Charlie, aren't you?'

'Oh yes.'

'And you feel sad about what he's going through.'

Punter nods.

'Now this problem of his, I wonder if it's to do with his health.'

'Yes. He's not well at all.'

'Bingo! First time lucky – well done, Lord. Excellent. Now, the Spirit says to you, that He will visit Charlie with hands of healing and raise him up from his bed of sickness, and Charlie will speak forth before the multitude and testify mightily to the Lord's bounties.'

'But he's a dog.'

'That's right, and you have an unclaimed gift of basket weaving. Well done. Next.'

You see the problem.

If you want to be a little more adventurous, here are some ideas:

'The coming days will be an exciting time, but unfortunately not for you. For you it'll just be one bunch of stuff after another, like normal.'

'Your anointed number is 5, your providentially blessed day is Tuesday, and your powerfully-claimed-in-the-Spirit food additive is E171.'

'I can't go into details, but you should wear shades, get your life insured, and avoid Albanians.'

The gift of healing

This must be the most popular gift of all, which I suppose shouldn't surprise us since it's the least spiritual. It is sad that people should find such bodily things as vanishing tumours and getting out of wheelchairs more exciting than words from the Lord and miraculous amounts of faith. Still, it's a good crowdpuller, I suppose.

I must admit that my own healing ministry has not been as spectacular as that of some big names you might know, and is largely focused on non-observable conditions and illnessess for which the person concerned was already receiving treatment. But this is just as important in its own way.

Remember that people suffering from serious health conditions are probably emotionally fragile and vulnerable, so make the best of this by having a huge dramatic healing meeting, with lots of big music and you shouting down a microphone at them about the power of the Lord, and you'll find them remarkably responsive to the things of the Spirit.

I also recommend having some helpers in the audience to cast away their crutches and walk, or shout, 'Praise the Lord, my halitosis has gone!' just to encourage the others. This may seem a bit dishonest, but it is only to get the ball rolling, and if it opens people up to the healing, I'm sure they'd be grateful in the long run.

The gift of faith

All Christians have faith, of course, and most of us are able to believe some pretty implausible things without any help from the Spirit. But to take on the vast unlikelihoods, contradictions and impossibilities of full Christian devotion requires supernatural gifting.

By this gift men (and women these days!) discard 'common sense' as the cloak of unrighteousness and the cagoule of unholiness. When by common sense the Enemy would have them cross the road to church at the lights, by faith alone they cover their eyes and step out against the flow and witness to the rapidly oncoming world by their miraculous preservation from fatal injury.

By the way, never let someone with the gift of faith set out the chairs for a prayer meeting. There's nothing more depressing than nine people meeting in a room that seats 420.

The gift of pictures

It's funny, isn't it, that in the days of the Old Testament, when the closest thing they had to movies was walking down a corridor in a pyramid watching two-dimensional dog-headed fellas and scantily clad servant girls go by on the wall, then God spoke to everyone in visions – all full of action, adventure and goats. Nowadays when we actually have movies everyone seems to get pictures from God instead. And who says God doesn't have a sense of humour?

The gift of discerning the spirits

This is a lovely gift that lets you see exactly what's wrong with everyone else and exorcise them into self-improvement. This is done by anointing them with oil and the laying on of hands, closely followed by the washing of hands. Here are the main spirits you'll have to deal with:

A spirit of unbelief

If any of your flock is wrong about something and still persists in error after you have put them right, then they have a spirit of unbelief. If, when you tell them this, they insist they haven't, then you have all the proof you need.

A spirit of apathy

This affects most Christians most of the time. Fortunately, it doesn't affect them very much, because it can't be bothered.

A spirit of heaviness

This is easy to spot but harder to solve. However, the RGA Ministries liturgical aerobics video *Casting the Stones* has been known to work wonders for the heaviness of believers. Unfortunately, its companion video *Eating the Stones*, about the St Hilda the Hermitess Diet, is currently unavailable for reasons of legal red tape.

Humility

This is hideously complicated. Have you got the gift of humility? If you think you have, it's a sure sign you haven't. If you know you aren't humble, then you probably are. The humbler you get, the more convinced you become that you haven't even started, so you have to try ever harder until you're infinitely humble and can never think of anything except how proud you are. Leave it be, is my advice. Don't be ashamed of being proud.

Stewardship

This is rarely recognized as a spiritual gift, because it is often confused with materialism, which is the secular equivalent. But do not neglect it, for it is meet and right for the true Church to demonstrate the Lord's favour by having comfy chairs, grand buildings and a cool sound system. How else can people recognize the Kingdom of God? Doeth not the Good Book say, 'Those who wait on the Lord can expect to be well tipped'? Or a good book, at least.

Ask the Rev.

The Lord has told me that I have the gift of raising the dead, which I'm very excited about. The problem is, I've got no one to try it out on. My friend Josh says I should have the faith to kill someone, so I can raise them again, as a glorious proof of the power of God. That sounds a bit scary. What do you think?

ALAN BARCODE

The Rev. says:
Yes, pretty scary. It's good that you're enthusiastic, but I find that trying to kill people rarely makes for successful evangelism. Why not start small? I'm sure you can find some wilted flowers to try to revive. If that works, you can move on to insects or something. If it doesn't, then try to develop a safer gift. I was very keen on stamps when I was your age.

How do I know if I've got the gift of knowledge?

STEPHEN OKAYEMBE

The Rev. says:
I have to say it doesn't sound like you have.

How to be pure

I once heard a true story about this church in some village which was doing everything right but just wasn't growing. So they sought the Lord about it. They sought him by day, and they sought him by night. And then in the morning they found him – he was everywhere, just as he always is, so that was nice. And he spake unto them, saying that the problem was that one of the leadership team was reading Harry Potter. So they threw him out, and shunned all contact with him – and the very next year a large Christian family moved into the area almost doubling the size of the congregation. The sinner soon moved away too, and all ended well.

This shows how important it is for anyone with a

ministry to keep themselves from all impurity, sin and taboos, so God can be with you. How do you expect to follow in the footsteps of heroes of the faith like David, Samson and Noah if your private life is compromised?

Here are the Rev's three steps to a sanctified lifestyle:

Vet your friends

Are friends and colleagues bringing non-Christian influences into your life? If you are in full-time ministry colleagues shouldn't be a problem – though you can never be too careful. But how many unsanctified friendships do you have? Think of all the time you spend being infected by their worldly attitudes, provocatively unbiblical clothing and seductively depraved lifestyles. Who knows what demonic swarms buzz around them unseen like an invisible cloud of hideous evil? Of course, if you look only skin deep they may seem sweet-natured and friendly, but probe beneath their outer appearance and you will find they're just waiting to lure you into unspeakable fornications, ultimately dragging you with them into a pit of filth and degradation. The Lord has long preserved me from the snares of friendship with the world, and I advise you to pursue the same gifting.

The one exception to this rule is if you run a course on friendship evangelism, when it becomes necessary to make friends with sinners to get a chance to tell them about God's love. I don't recommend it, though. The only time we tried the friendship strategy at St U's we got one convert but lost three. I've done more unsuccessful evangelism in my time than the Devil's had hot dinners, but this is the only time I ever had a net loss.

Vet the world

Each time you step out of your front door, you take your soul in your hands. The earth is full of temptations and pollutions lurking in the most innocent-looking places. Only last week I found some very evil influences in a tin of corned beef at the Co-op and in the Brockley Cross mini-roundabout. Your home is your hermitage. The Christian ideal is to stay indoors for ever if possible, without TV and books, going out only to look at God's lovely sunsets and wearing a protective body bag.

Staying indoors is one of the most underrated strategies for avoiding the wiles of the Enemy, allowing you to devote all your time to developing a healthier spirituality – depending on whom you stay indoors with, of course.

Vet yourself

Whether all this works, however, depends on how sound your homelife is. Let's take a look, shall we?

Television

I must insist that as a man of God (or woman these days!), you should watch nothing on secular TV but the news and under-5s programming. I take the corrupting power of TV so seriously I have an ongoing ministry of prayer and complaining about it, which unfortunately means I have to watch an awful lot of it, so you don't have to.

If this sounds restrictive, you don't realise how much wonderful Christian TV there is to watch. I heartily recommend the Righteousness Channel: all you need to get it is a holy bowl and a lot of faith. And some money. It offers sound and sanctified alternatives to all the most popular shows.

Favourites include *Winner Loses All*, the theological quiz where the last shall be first and the contestant who makes the least effort to win gets the prize – a heightened sense of spiritual well-being. Confusing, but biblical. My own talk show, *Gerald*, lets you the public expose your spiritual problems in a degrading craving for 4 minutes of microcelebrity, while I sort it all out for you with a word of encouragement.

In *Changing Sanctuaries*, churches like St Francis Xavier's, Putney, tart up churches like Bank Street Strict Baptist Chapel, while the Bank Street Boys burn down St F's. My own favourite show is *Sinstoppers*, where top clergy appeal for help in identifying major transgressors, featuring reconstructions and CCTV footage of vice and iniquity in a tasteful and useful way.

And there's a whole parallel universe of kiddies' shows for parents seeking to bring their family up in the Lord. *The Patient Gang* are always getting into scrapes, but endure them cheerfully. *Uncle Trevor's Wacky Wardrobe* explains basic theological concepts with the help of some talking clothes. *The Bibletubbies* are fluffy fellows who can only speak in tongues and live in an underground bunker for fear of Armageddon, but who come out sometimes to skip about in the fields and see baby Jesus smiling down on them from the sky.

With such a love feast of alternative reality TV to enjoy and learn from, there's really no excuse for being a part of the secular culture of this lost world.

Videos

I have known whole families fearsomely oppressed from forces unleashed by a single children's film about the occult called *The Lion, the Witch and the Wardrobe*, so be equally careful here. I cautiously recommend Vatican Video who do some great theological blockbusters like *Mission Infallible* and *Papal Attraction*, but only if you also get my *Vatican videos study guide*, which points out where these well-meaning papists have been led into error.

Newspapers

If you let unsaved voices tell you what's going on, your outlook will be skewed and you'll go right off the altar rails. I find that *The High Pentecostal-Reformed Last Days Clarion*, *Judgmentalism Today* and the *South London Godbotherer* give me all the information about the contemporary world that I need (i.e. none at all), plus meaty theological debate within acceptable parameters, kosher recipes and the glossolalia crossword, with very little delusion or titillation of any kind.

Music

If you listen to secular music with provocative beats and lyrics about profane feelings, you can never expect to live a life empowered unto mighty works. We are blessed in my neck of the woods to have Divine FM Christian radio so that serious Christians can spend their lives in wall-to-wall worship, interspersed with inspiring items like the daily meditation with Dr June Bubbly, which admittedly would work better, I think, if she could meditate aloud. They also have lovely current affairs discussion programmes where the presenters desperately try to persuade their guests to argue with each other.

If you find yourself unable to make the leap from the sounds of Sodom to a diet of pure hymnology in one go, you could try to wean yourself off it with Christian pop. Our own worship group at St U's is currently recording a CD called *The Redeemed Beatles*, recapturing those fab songs with purified lyrics, all arranged for acoustic guitar and flute. It includes 'Here Comes the Son', 'Do You Want to Know a Curate?', 'She's Leaving Rome', and 'Back in the UCCF'. If everything else they've ever done is anything to go by, it will be unspeakably awful, but I thought I ought to mention it.

* * *

The Rev. Testifies

A couple of years ago I appointed Sibling Peter Crucible as deacon for spiritual warfare, with a mandate to sniff out witches, relocate territorial spirits, and alert the church to the latest trends and developments in the world of evil. He had not been in office long before he came running to me with horrifying news about a bestselling book for both adults and children that contained witchcraft, child sacrifice, orgies, demons and page after page of the most deviant sex and violence. Worst of all, many members of the church had been reading it.

I sent him to gather the entire membership for an extraordinary church meeting, with all their copies, while I lit the bonfire. At the meeting he gave a big dramatic speech and got everyone to bring their copies forward. It was the Bible.

"I think we've all learned something important today, haven't we, Rev?" he said with smug solemnity. So I put him on the bonfire instead. Because take it from me, if there's one thing in this world worse than demonic corruption and perverted filth, it's a smartarse.

* * *

Going deeper

Now, I realize that many of you will be thinking, 'What you say doesn't make sense to me, Rev. Gerald. All that you have prescribed is how I live my life naturally. And yet still I find myself assaulted with impure thoughts about underwear or not going to the half night of prayer for local government spending policy, and still my ministry flounders on the rocks of not being terribly good. How are the demons getting through?'

The answer is food, sibling. Are you not feeding your very flesh, blood, brains and other bits, with food made by fallen, godless worldlings?

'But', you say, 'where can we get pure and holy food, unpolluted by the evil hands of unbelievers?'

I'm glad you asked: the Rev. Gerald Ambulance Sanctified Supermarket. Every product is baked, picked, packed, whatever, by truly born-of-the-blood believers. May the Lord deal with me, be it ever so severely, if our cows are milked by anyone but biblically baptized, Spirit-filled virgins who have signed a statement of faith and cover their heads at all times. You can get everything from new wines and holy spirits (non-alcoholic) to paschal lamb chops, and from immaculate conception olive oil to our famous Trinity sundae.

Verily in these days the words of the prophet Isaiah are being fulfilled that say, 'Come, buy milk and grape juice, without money and without cost.' (I think that last bit is picture language.)

Ask the Rev.

When I look out at my congregation, and all their vacant, gormless faces, I often get the urge to go down and smack them. How do I know if this is an impure thought, or from the Lord?

REV. CLIFF TASKER

The Rev. says:
All urges, Sibling Cliff, are from the Lord. He's the one who made us, after all. But some are sent as temptations to resist, some are just his way of telling you to have a good time, and some are temptations to succumb to so that he can justly damn you, because you're a godless reprobate. How can you tell the difference? See where you get sent on the day of judgement.

Just about everything is impure if you look into it enough. My advice is never do anything, or don't look into it too much.

Sorry if that's not much help, but I've just spent an appallingly depressing evening listening to the choir's dress rehearsal of *A Very Reggae Christmas*, so in the circumstances it's better than you deserve. In fact, now I think of it, why not go ahead and beat up your congregation, and if you feel a ministry developing, I could offer you many exciting opportunities to work at your calling here at St Ursula's.

I really believe the Lord is telling me to stop going to school, because all the other kids are filthy godless worldlings, and because my science teacher promotes false lies of Satan about the big bang and evolution. I've told my mum, and she just says, 'Yeah, right'.

How can I convince her that I am taking a saintly stand against false teaching, and not just skiving?

PHIL JUMBLY

The Rev. says:

The best way to convince her would be to stay at school as a light in the darkness and salt in the blandness, but counteract the infection of false teaching by extra orthodox studies in your spare time. How does that grab you?

I recommend *6000 Years of Matter: Science for Home Schoolers.* It is an ultra-sound course in creation science by Hank Moron, covering biology, chemistry, physics, astrophysics and cosmology, all from information contained in Genesis, Psalms and other scriptural authorities.

Have you got the anointment?

But enough about me, let's have a look at you. Are you an anointed saint destined for a world-famous, miraculous, soul-saving ministry? Or a no-hoper who should donate his dog collar to Battersea Dogs' Home?

Find out with the Rev. Gerald Discernmentographical Questionnaire, which will work out your anointment to the nearest whole number. Pick one answer for each question, and work out your score from the bit at the end entitled 'How To Work Out Your Score'. Not too complicated for you, is it?

1 What is your favourite music?
(a) *Let Me Be a Living Mountain* by Tim Splendid.

(b) Mass by Giovanni Pierluigi da Palestrina.

(c) *Sympathy for the Devil* by the Rolling Stones.

(d) The choirs of angels who sing me to sleep.

2 You buy a Mars bar and get too much change. What do you do?

(a) Keep it.

(b) Go back and give them the money.

(c) Keep going back to the shop in case it happens again.

(d) Why would I waste money on chocolate when it does nothing for my soul?

3 Which version of the Bible do you read most?

(a) The Special Up-to-Date Compulsory for Everybody Version (with the sunset on the front).

(b) The original Greek, Hebrew and Aramaic.

(c) The what?

(d) None, I know it off by heart.

4 What is your favourite drink?

(a) A nice cup of tea.

(b) Transubstantiated non-alcoholic communion grape juice.

(c) Whatever gets me smashed quickest.

(d) The new wine of the Spirit.

5 If you had the gift of tongues, what would you do?

(a) Keep quiet about it.

(b) Spend two hours a day praying in the Spirit.

(c) Try it out on the cute girl/bloke next door.

(d) Shout, 'Full house!'

6 When I pray...

(a) I feel better;

(b) the church gives me a standing ovation;

(c) I fall asleep;

(d) the earth moves, the dead rise and the heavens open.

7 If you could have one prayer answered, it would be for...

(a) chocolate;

(b) peace and justice throughout the world;

(c) no one else's prayers to be answered;

(d) what are you talking about? All my prayers are answered.

8 Do you believe there is one special person somewhere for you?

(a) Yes, the Angel Gabriel told me so, but I'm waiting for them to get the message too.

(b) No, I am committed to a life of celibacy.

(c) Yes, and I'll try out everyone till I find out who it is.

(d) Yes, it's Jesus.

9 I sing hymns...

(a) with my hands in the air;

(b) with my legs in the air;

(c) once a year outside Woolworth's to get money for Christmas prezzies;

(d) with a deep sense of inner reverence.

10 Going down the high street, you see a group from a nearby church preaching from a box to passers-by. What do you do?

(a) Give them a secret Christian smile.

(b) Set up a rival box and explain why their pre-tribulation rapture theology is up the spout, and how to really be saved.

(c) Run into Gap and hide in the changing rooms till it's all over.

(d) Listen for a while, then pretend to get converted to encourage everyone else.

11 If I were the Pope, I would...
   (a) give all my riches to the poor;
   (b) wear big dresses and a skull cap (why rock the boat?);
   (c) try out my papal infallibility on the lottery;
   (d) I am the Pope.

12 It is infallibly revealed unto you that there is one day till the end of the world. How do you spend your last 24 hours?
   (a) Credit card shopping.
   (b) Prayer and meditation.
   (c) Boozing. (Hangover in the morning? I don't think so.)
   (d) Running up and down the high street with a sandwich board and a loud-speaker.

13 You pray that everything will be all right while you're away at the Union of Famous Christians annual conference. You come home to find your house under three feet of water. How do you react?
   (a) Shout at God.
   (b) Trust that all will work out for the best in the long run for those who have eyes to see it, and thank the Lord for a new sermon illustration.
   (c) Flood your neighbours' houses to make yourself feel better.
   (d) Walk on the water, preach to the spectators and baptize all your converts in the water.

14 You get carried away and preach for two and a half hours on 'Making Time for God'. Your congregation...
  (a) think they've died and gone to heaven;
  (b) wish they'd died and gone to heaven;
  (c) wish they'd died and gone to somewhere with fewer preachers;
  (d) would be quite happy if you kept going till they died.

How to work out your score

Score one point for every (a), two for every (b), minus one for every (c), and three for every (d).

If you scored over 42

Congratulations, you scored more than mathematically possible! Unfortunately this means you cheated. Go forth in shame and penitence.

If you scored 42

Maximum score! Either you are the next Rev. Gerald Ambulance, or you are Rev. Gerald Ambulance. Why are you wasting your time reading this book, when you could be turning loaves into fishes and claiming extraterrestrial civilizations for Christ?

If you scored 32–41

You have the anointment, sibling. You exude an inspiring, even nauseating level of holiness, and would have been at home in the Bible. On good days you hover two centimetres off the ground, and you really just bring a really real blessing to everyone. Really. I could go on, but you might start losing points for pride.

If you scored 18–31

You have it in you to be a great man of God (or woman these days!). Hide not thy saltiness under a bushel, sibling, but let it flow forth for the healing of the nation. You need to beef up your spirituality a bit, though, to claim that full anointment. Have a look through the RGA Ministries catalogue to find the everlasting lifestyle essentials that will make up the shortfall, from blessingnosis tapes to Rev. Gerald action figures.

If you scored 9–17

I'm afraid you're a bit unanointed, aren't you? You're a bona fide saint, but also a bona fide sinner. Which is only natural, but when you're supposed to be a purveyor of the supernatural that's not really good enough, is it? Are you really trying? If you are, you must learn to let go and let God. If not, then what do you expect, you idle waster?

If you scored 0–8

The good news, sibling, is that your life is a whole bundle of stuff for God to improve. The bad news is that until he does, you shouldn't be let loose on the righteous flock of Ephraim until you understand the difference between shepherd and butcher. Since you wouldn't know the difference between God's will and pigswill, let me direct you to take a pilgrimage to Lewisham in sackcloth and ashes or Lycra cycling shorts, whichever you find more humiliating, and check into St Ursula's clerical rehabilitation programme for some intensive ministry.

If you scored under 0

Uh oh! You're a sin blackspot, and not in a nice sense. May the locusts of Moab devour thy progeny, thou unclean publican! Unto thee will the Scriptures be fulfilled that say 'Woe!'

Bonus humility test

Give yourself the mark out of ten you think you deserve, subtract that number from ten, and the number you get is your score.

Valediction

As we draw to the close of what I am sure you will agree has been a truly beatitudinous outpouring (or 'good book' for those of you whose vocabulary is not yet fully sanctified), may I say what a great privilege it has been for you to read it. But let not the glory go unto me who am but a loin to issue forth the fruit of divine pronouncements.

If your ministry has been blessed by this mighty work, why not buy a copy for everyone you know, preach sermons on it, and write worship songs about it? Any publicity at all, really. Not that earthly glory means anything to me in my singleminded pursuit of celestial fame and the humiliation of my vile wormy flesh, but the work of the Kingdom really could use the money.

If you are ever in Lewisham, do come by the Manse. My door is always open to fellow spiritual celebrities to exchange mission strategies, insights and anecdotes. Or anyone, really. It can get rather lonely in this job sometimes. No nutters, though.

After reading of all that true ministry could and should be, you may feel irredeemably unanointed, as if God could not possibly want you worrying his sheep any longer, and that you might as well return to the life of amateur Christianity under a deep dark cloud of judgement and condemnation. Good idea. You'll probably want to come along to St Ursula's, where the ministry is never below five-star. Here's what to do:

If you have been converted to the full truth of the High Pentecostal-Reformed faith

Please do come along on Sunday morning. We currently meet, for reasons I'm not prepared to go into, in a disused nuclear bunker behind the car park of Lewisham Tesco's, where we gather together to bear witness in word, worship and wobbling. (Men may mock (and women these days!), but if negotiations with Toronto Airport Christian Fellowship and HTB come off, this could be the next big thing.)

We meet at the sacred hour of 10.30, but you ought to get there by 9.00, because you'll be asked to complete a thorough discernmentographical questionnaire on your beliefs and lifestyle.

If you pass, you'll receive a warm welcome, a membership certificate and a small three-volume book on the kind of conduct, clothing, hairstyle, language, church attendance, tithing, obedience, reading, friends, eating, etc. that the Lord now expects of you, entitled *The Meaning of Free Grace*.

If you fail, then depending on the score you'll either be asked to leave so we can purify the building in time for the service, or burned.

If you haven't

Don't.